William Staats

A Tight Squeeze

The Adventures of a Gentleman

William Staats

A Tight Squeeze
The Adventures of a Gentleman

ISBN/EAN: 9783744676274

Printed in Europe, USA, Canada, Australia, Japan

Cover: Foto ©Thomas Meinert / pixelio.de

More available books at **www.hansebooks.com**

A TIGHT SQUEEZE;

OR,

THE ADVENTURES OF A GENTLEMAN,

WHO, ON A WAGER OF TEN THOUSAND DOLLARS.
UNDERTOOK TO GO FROM NEW YORK TO
NEW ORLEANS IN THREE WEEKS,
WITHOUT MONEY,

AS A PROFESSIONAL TRAMP.

By· "STAATS."

BOSTON:
LEE AND SHEPARD, PUBLISHERS.
NEW YORK:
CHARLES T. DILLINGHAM.
1879.

Stereotyped by C. C. Morse & Son,
Haverhill, Mass.

CONTENTS.

CHAPTER I.

A TIGHT SQUEEZE.

CHAPTER I.

THE PRODIGAL AND THE WAGER.

"WASSON, what is a *tramp?*"
"Dunno."
"Cleveland, what is a *tramp?*"
No answer.
"Wasson, accommodate me, if you please, by introducing the extremity of your boot to Mr. Cleveland."
"Ouch! What in thunder are you kicking me for, Wasson?"
"I'm not kicking you; extremes meet, my boy, and there was a natural repulsion. Hough wants to know what a tramp is!"
"How do I know! Ah! here comes Smythe; he will tell you."
"Ah, Smythe, my boy, just in time! Wasson don't know any thing, and Cleveland won't tell what he does know; what's a tramp?" There now — that's a good fellow — don't open your mouth so; you'll injure your neck, — just tell me all you know about them."

(9)

" What's a which ? Tramp ! "

" Don't be a poll parrot, Smythe. Tell me what they are. You've been to college and learned to row, and box, and play base ball, and ought to know nearly every thing. Here I am continually reading about them. Every paper you pick up is full of them. Tramp, *tramp*, TRAMP, from one end of the paper to the other. There is not a chicken purloined off a roost ; a man killed ; a house fired ; a train ditched ; virtue outraged, vice embellished, or deviltry of any kind perpetrated, but this omnipresent scape-goat of the nineteenth century appears to be at the bottom of it all. Now I want to know what a tramp is."

"I am sorry that I cannot enlighten you, Hough, but — "

" But," exclaimed Wasson, interrupting Smythe, " if I am not very much mistaken, here comes a gentleman who can ! " And as the lawn gate swung to its place, with a clang of the latch, there appeared walking up the gravelled walk, a being, whose every square inch of superficial surface indicated a *bona fide*, unadulterated specimen of the genus vagabond.

A frock coat, — guiltless of buttons, (save the two in the rear, where they were of no earthly use) — with half a frock gone, and the remainder of the garment mottled like unto the celebrated garment that got Joseph in a hole, was fastened at the neck with a glittering horse-shoe nail. A pair of pants, fantastically fringed with ragged ends about their extremities, higher up bore the brands of many a camp-fire. Their original color had long since struck to the over-powering allied forces of wind and weather, mud and grease.

In a landscape they might have looked a subdued maroon, etched with lampblack. Below the fantastic fringe work appeared a pair of feet encased in a boot and a shoe. The shoe had evidently seen better days, and seemed to shrink with humiliated pride from the forced companionship of the boot, which was a plebeian of the Stogie family. The shoe was long, narrow and pointed. The boot was coarse, thick and stubby. The toe of the boot had an air-hole in it, extending clean across the upper. The shoe was intact, and had a brass buckle the size of a door plate, which give it an air of fallen greatness. But the boot was in proud possession of a heel, while the shoe had none, equalizing matters. In glaring contrast to this tatterdemalion attire, the hat, that completed the picture, was a new straw affair, and looked like a bright, fresh, shingle roof, clapped on a very dilapidated, old building. The face beneath the hat was round and plump, very dirty, quite keen, frescoed with tobacco juice and embossed with a short, stumpy beard. As the figure drew nigh the group on the lawn, boot, shoe, pants, coat and face seemed to blend into an animated object, while the bran new hat kept calling out, like a side-show man on a fair ground, " Here we are ! Now you have us ! An epitome of Hard Times ! A parody on financial acumen ! A caricature on the fat of the land ! What aint rags is dirt, and what aint dirt is bugs ! We're the remnant of other days ! We're the breaking-up-of-a-hard-win- ter ! We're a pariah, a scavenger, an outcast ! That's what we are, and we want you to know it. Here's your prodigal for you ! Kill your fatted calf of kitchen fag-ends and serve up the banquet on the back door step. Bring out the purple and fine linen of your ragbags. Here's your prodigal, and he's come back hungry ! "

But though the hat said this, as plain as a hat could, the figure beneath the hat spoke quite differently. Having, with a faltering step and a pronounced limp in the shoe foot, approached the four gentlemen who were enjoying their after dinner cigars on the lawn, the figure with a keen, swift glance took an inventory of each person before him, and then pulling off the new hat — to the great joy of a lot of hair that appeared relieved from the constraints of good society — it said, in a mumbling voice :

" Gentlemen, this is the saddest moment of my life. I am no professional beggar, but the victim of misfortunes, and reduced from comfort to my present state of want by calamities over which I had no control. If you could give me some assistance it would be a great blessing to me, and a noble act for you ; for I have not had a bite to eat for *four days*, and my clothes would drop off of me with starvation if they were not falling off from raggedness."

" Four days ! " exclaimed all.

" Four days," solemnly reasserted the figure.

" And you still live ! " said Hough.

" I still live," returned the figure, as solemnly as before, but with a shrewd, covert little glance at Hough accompanying the answer.

Wasson noticed the glance, and laughed. Cleveland looked up and the prodigal greeted him with a benignant smile. Smythe withdrew his hands from their repose in his pockets, and, with open mouth, gazed first at the patrician shoe, then at the plebeian boot, then at the subdued, maroon colored, landscape pants, then at the skirtless coat, and at last fastened his attention on the fascination of the brilliant, galvanized-iron, horse-shoe nail.

" Are — are you a — TRAMP ? "

" No, Sir ! " emphatically and indignantly replied the prodigal.

" Then we're lost ! " exclaimed all four, and Hough continued, " Had you been a tramp I'd have given you a dollar."

The prodigal looked surprised — a trifle suspicious. For the first time in his life he found his vagabondage quoted at a premium.

" Gentlemen," he said, " pardon me if my native modesty prompted me to deny the truth. I will confess that, having spent my substance in assisting the miseries of others, I am, through the fault of my own generosity and moral rectitude, at last brought to that sad phase of mortal existence comprehended by the name " tramp." I *am* a tramp — and I do not say it boastingly — ; Heaven forbid ! " And with a smile of ineffable sweetness, in which dirt and " native modesty " were harmoniously blended, the prodigal meekly folded his hands and rolled his eyes skywards.

" Found, at last ! " exclaimed all.

The incidents of this chapter occurred one sunny August afternoon, on the lawn in front of Smythe's summer cottage on Long Island Sound, not far from the lovely little village of Greenwich.

Smythe's cottage was a pretty little piece of carpenter work in the Swiss chatelet style — so delightfully expensive and romantic.

Algernon Smythe was the son of his father. A
clear understanding of this matter is necessary inas-
much as the ancestral Smythes bore the name of
Smith, and the one immediately preceding Algernon
had *his* "Smith" decorated with the prefix Josiah.
Josiah Smith drifted away from the cobble stones of
Connecticut — where the *Smith* family had long been
at warfare with the rocks about the possession of a
few acres of sterile, sorrel-trodden, ground, — at an
early age, and found his way to New York city.
With him came the customary solitary shilling. But
this *Smith* shilling was an inflationist. It swelled itself into houses and lots, and stocks and bonds, and
shaved notes and fore-closed mortgages, and fifty per
cent. premiums on seven per cent loans, and kept itself so busily employed that when Josiah Smith retired from active life and took up a permanent resi-
dence in Greenwood, his only son and heir found
himself sole master of a million of money. This was
too much wealth to be comfortably worn by the name
of Smith. Why, Algernon could remember when he
was a little fellow, sanding sugar and dusting spices
in his father's store, familiar little boys, — who were
manœuvering for raisins, — used to affectionately call
him "Smiffy!"

As a consequence when Algernon returned from
Paris (*Pahree* he called it) he no longer intruded the
private "i" into the public eye, but put a "y" in
place of it. Then, that his name might be parted in

the middle, — to match his hair, — he tapered off the
"i"-less creation with an "e"; adopted a coat of
arms ; selected a motto ; wanted to know if Connecticut was not somewhere in Massachusetts "you
know " ; always said *brava!* at the opera ; and bought
him a yacht!

Of the other guests at the cottage ; Mr. Hough
was the relative appendage of a City Savings Bank.
He drew $3,500 per annum from the bank and sev-
eral thousand from other sources. Mr. Wasson was
generally supposed to be an artist. He was always
going to have a picture finished for the next exhibition. "A thing that Church or Bierstadt might be
proud of." Meanwhile a doting father, who, in a distant Massachusetts town, had first made shoes on his
own knees, but now made them on the knees of some
five hundred of his fellow men, kindly furnished him
with a liberal means of subsistence until his profession was established on a paying basis.

Benjamin Cleveland was a young fellow, but little
more than twenty-three. His mother had belonged
to an old Boston family.

When Ben was ten years old his widowed mother
died leaving him to the tender care of his uncle, with
a legacy of twenty thousand dollars. By means of
this inheritance he had obtained liberal educational
advantages, — attaining his majority shortly after
graduating (without any honors) at Yale. (Boston-
ians take honors at Harvard.) After leaving college
he diligently applied himself to the problem of life.
He had determined upon making his mark in the
world. Nearly all young men do so determine. Tho

"mark" up to the opening of this narrative was
neither a very prominent or promising one. On his
twenty-first birth-day his uncle, who neither understood or sympathized with him, — in fact rather dis-
liked him, — paid into Ben's hands $15,450, the re-
mainder of the legacy left by his mother, and bade
him " God speed " ; — a fashion some people have of
shifting on to God's shoulders responsibilities that belong on their own. For a couple of years Ben enjoyed himself looking around among his fellow men,
and at the age of twenty-three had $10,400 left to his
bank account. He was fond of good living, fond of
adventure, fond of sport, fond of being his own master, fond of a congenial laziness, and fond of every
thing pertaining to good health save hum-drum work,
and money making by the "plod" process. He could
lie on his back and build castles in the air all day
long. But it is doubtful if he would have undertaken
the exertion of going twenty rods to get one of the
foundation stones to commence one of his castles with.
He was something of a *dreamer.* Not much of a
doer. He ignored the past; enjoyed the present;
neglected the future.

Several moments elapsed in silence, while the lawn
party surveyed the *rara-avis* before them. The prodigal was the first to speak. Extending his hand toward Hough, he suggestively remarked, " Where are
you, boss ? "

" Here is your dollar," replied Hough, presenting
him one; "you have earned it, my friend, by your
truthfulness. Now, my friend, tell me what a tramp
is ? "

"Why, a tramp's a tramp," replied the prodigal.

"Concise, if not lucid," remarked Wasson.

"Yes, but *what* are they, who are they, where are they, what do they do and where do they go ?" persisted Hough.

The prodigal quietly picked a gravel stone out of the gaping toe of the boot, and answered, "They're *tramps;* that's what they are. Dead-brokes; bums; beats; codjers; hand-out solicitors; cross-tie sailors; free-lunch fiends; centennial rangers; square-meal crusaders! They're everywhere, they do every thing, and go all over. They're the great American travellers of the nineteenth century. Explorers. Progressionists. Agrarians. I'm one of 'em myself, I am! I'm just from New Orleans, and going to Boston," and the prodigal stopped to request a donation of tobacco.

"But where do they live?" asked Wasson.

"Great Blazes! They live where they eat! What a question!" And the prodigal completely annihilated poor Wasson by rolling his eyes upon him in supreme astonishment.

"Yes, but what do they eat? You know they must eat, or they would not live;" and Smythe felt that he had cornered him.

"True for you sir. Well they eat mostly at different places. When in New York some of them like to stop at the Astor, and others again prefer rooming in the lumber piles and taking their meals at Delmonico's. The Fifth Avenue is good enough for me though;" and he smiled upon Smythe, and Algernon opened his eyes and mouth to their fullest extent.

"Don't you ever work? Do you never care to earn money at labor?" asked Wasson.

"Work! Labor! Me! I'm not used to it, but I don't stand back from it on that account. No sir. I love to work. Do you know of any body that wants a hand to help cut ice, or can strawberries, or take astronomical observations? If you do, tell me, for I'm their man. Work! I *adore* it!" and his face expressed his adoration.

"How long did it take you to come from New Orleans?" asked Hough.

The prodigal studied a moment, and then replied, "I left New Orleans on the 20th of last month. I made St. Louis in eight days and it's taken me two weeks and a trifle more to come from St. Louis here."

"Why, that is over one hundred miles a day! You're a fast walker," said Hough.

"Walk! Who said any thing about walking? Not much. I walked when I felt like it, and I rode when I felt like it."

"You had money, then?" asked Wasson.

"Money!" exclaimed he of the maroon pants, disdainfully. "Money! Nary red. What did I want of money. Any fool can travel with money. I beat my way!" and a look of conscious pride illumined his face.

"Came from New Orleans here in three weeks, without any money!" And the magnitude of the undertaking so overwhelmed Mr. Smythe that he viewed the tramp as a second Humboldt.

"Step around to the kitchen and tell them to give you something to eat."

"No, I'm obliged to you, stranger. I just had two squares and three hand-outs, and I couldn't eat another morsel. I'm sorry, but such is the fact," replied the prodigal to the utter neglect of his assertion that for four days he had not tasted food.

When Wasson reminded him of it, he coolly remarked that it was true enough, and arose from his having a terrible toothache that prevented his tasting any thing.

"I must tear myself from you, gentlemen," he continued. "Time is precious, and although I enjoy your society, I must not neglect business. I'm much obliged for the dollar, mister. I'll spend it usefully and judiciously. Ta, ta!" and with a free and easy wave of his hand, the tramp turned and walked jauntily down the gravelled walk without the slightest sign of the limp he entered with.

After his departure Hough broke out in a boisterous fit of hilarity.

"That's a *tramp!*" he exclaimed. "We have seen the elephant, now, gentlemen, what do *you* think of him?"

"What a supreme amount of *chic!*" said Smythe, whom, it will be remembered, had been to Paris.

"Grand! Glorious! It's a fortune to him!" replied Hough, feigning to be lost in admiration. And Cleveland said, meditatively,

"Three thousand miles in three weeks without a cent! By Jove!"

But Wasson rejoined that he did not believe a word of it.

"It can't be done," said Smythe, positively. "No man could do it. *I* couldn't do it myself!"

"Yes it *can* be done," cried Cleveland, " whether *you* could do it or not. *I* could do it."

" You!"

" Yes, *me!* "

" I'd be willing to give you three months, and wager that then you could not. You'd starve to death in three days, and commence telegraphing us to come and bring you home before you crossed New Jersey," said Smythe, contemptuously deriding the idea of Cleveland's undertaking the feat.

" Don't be too sure about that, Smythe," retorted Cleveland, warming up. " What man has done, man can do. If that fellow came from New Orleans here in a little over three weeks without a cent, I can go from here to New Orleans in the same time on a like amount of money. I'll wager ten thousand dollars I can do it!" And Mr. Benjamin Cleveland arose to his feet and nodded his head in an aggressive manner, though he had not the remotest idea his challenge would be accepted, and only made the boast to support his assertion. Great then was his surprise — and a surprise not untinctured with consternation, when Smythe quickly replied, "I take the bet. Hough, Wasson, you heard Ben. It's a bargain. When will you start, Cleveland?"

But Ben courageously backed his assertion by quickly replying,

" To-morrow!"

" Pshaw! Cleveland, don't make a fool of yourself," spoke up Wasson. " Even if that fellow did really do as he says he did, remember, he is a *professional tramp*, and you would be but a novice, at best. You will lose your money, sure."

"I'm not urgent about the matter, only I do not like a man to be so positive about a thing he knows nothing of. You can draw the wager if you wish, Ben," said Smythe.

The manner in which he said it, however, nettled Ben, and though he had made his wager thoughtlessly, and without a consideration of the humiliations, privations, and hardships embraced in the proposed feat, he refused to retract.

"No, Smythe. . I don't take water. The bet is made. Let it stand."

There was a peculiar stubbornness in Ben's nature that compelled him after having made a boast to carry it out. Besides, the proposition was attractive from its startling novelty. It was an excitement his nature craved. In the quick communion of his mind the following thoughts resolved themselves into argumentative forces. "I'm a worthless, shiftless, good-for-nothing fellow anyway. I'm not rich enough to support the life I would like to lead, and I know nothing about 'money-making.' I need a good, practical knowledge of the world more than any thing else in it. A good shaking up. How to obtain it I don't know. There are undoubtedly thousands of channels open, but they are hidden from me. I have $10,400. If I lose my wager, I am young and the world is before me. If I win, I'll have enough to take me to Europe and see the sights for a couple of years. At all events, there are none interested save myself. I am alone in the world; none dependent on me, I'm dependent on none. Responsible to no one for my acts, — none to console a misfortune — nor to share a triumph. I'll go!"

And go he did.

By the terms of the wager, duly drawn up that evening, Cleveland was to start from the City Hall, in New York City, at six o'clock in the afternoon of the 10th of September, without money or any thing of value on his person. In this condition he was to make his way to St. Louis and from there to New Orleans, at which last named city he was to arrive, (and make known his arrival by a telegram from the St. Charles Hotel,) at, or before ten o'clock, A. M., City Hall time, October the 2d, making the tramp in twenty-one days from New York, with four hours *grace* on the 2d of October, thrown in at the suggestion of Hough. It was further stipulated that at no time while performing the feat, should he appeal for aid to friends, or use the influences of relatives or name, either by reference or application, to assist him. To recapitulate : — Benjamin Cleveland was to make his way from New York to New Orleans, via St. Louis, in three weeks, as a penniless, professional TRAMP ! "

CHAPTER II.

THE START.

ON the 10th of September, the four friends had a final meeting at a sumptuous little dinner, given at the Fourteenth Street Delmonico's, by Smythe. At three o'clock in the afternoon the party broke up, with one last toast to the success of our friend's undertaking.

As the hands of the City Hall clock pointed the hour of six that evening, Smythe, Hough, and Wasson, with a number of friends who had been informed of the wager, shook hands with Ben on the steps of the City Hall and bade him *bon voyage*. A minute after, when the hives of the great metropolis were turning loose their human bees, and the streets were swarming with released humanity, homeward bound, Benjamin Cleveland walked down Courtlandt Street, with his hands in his empty pockets — feeling as he never felt before in all his life — A TRAMP !   *   *   *

Reader were you ever " broke " ? Do you remember ever to have found yourself without money and without the possibility of getting it ? If so, you will not surely have to tax your memory to recall the cir-

cumstance. The feeling of utter helplessness you
then experienced will be indelibly stamped on your
mind —fresh and green for a life time. You were in
the world, yet not of it. You were a part and parcel
of humanity, yet held nothing in common with it.
Your mind wandered from subject to subject, and from
proposition to proposition, in a dazed, uncontrolled
manner that left your physical nature without a guide.
How empty every thing seemed. All you met appeared to look right into your pockets and discover
the horrible truth. The commonest mortal with a
home and an occupation became a prince of peace and
plenty in your eyes. And then the ever occurring,
never answered, eternally harassing question that was
constantly forcing itself upon you in a thousand
shapes, " What shall I do ? " You truly felt how
small, petty and insignificant a thing man is without
money. A nonentity ; a cipher ; a NOTHING ! A
shadow of existence — an effigy of immortality.
Then the desperate thoughts that came ploughing
along, tumbling over one another, and frantically ap-
pealing to you, for the action you did not possess.
Was it not horrible ! The dark deeds that pictured
themselves to you. The wild promptings to some desperate act. How you *hated* your fellow man. *He
was not your fellow man !* He was a being belonging
to altogether a different sphere than yours. There
was no fellowship about it. You were an Ishmaelite,
and there was a savage satisfaction in feeling that all
the world had its hand raised against you, and yours
against all the world. Indeed, to tell the truth, you
were not far from desperate deeds. The step from

poverty to crime is a short one,— if poverty, *itself*, be
not a crime. A man without money feels an ownership in every one else's property. An ownership
where Might becomes the agent of Possession. You
felt it. And perhaps it was more a lack of opportunity than inclination that kept you from becoming a
criminal. Then do you remember the vows you made,
" if you could only once get out of this fix!" The
vices you intended to shun ; the economy you would
practice ; the practical and substantial sympathy you
would have for all forlorn mortals in your present predicament? The virtues of industry, perseverance
and prudence you would religiously follow?
Bah!

" When the devil was sick, the devil a saint would be.
When the devil got well, the devil a saint was he."

But perchance you have been " broke " more than
once. Several times it may be. Vices, carelessness
and a peculiar faculty for getting rid of money have
reduced you to the predicament frequently. It has
become normal. Do you dread it? No. It has lost
its horrors. You have discovered that a man who
starves in this country commits suicide. You have
also learned how to let your self respect have a half-
holiday. Rags have become familiar to you and wear
easily. You have learned to ask that you may receive. To knock at the door that the purse of the
party within may be opened unto you. And, withal,
there is a sort of freedom in the situation that is
agreeable. The conventionalities of society have no
claim upon you. You are beholden to no one, and
no one to you. As free as the winds to come and

go, work or play, sing or howl — in fact, *to do as you
please!* Stocks up or stocks down — it is all the
same. Banks may go into liquidation, and insurance
companies only insure a loss. What do you care?
The president may go to Canada and the cashier to
Europe, and all available funds go along with them.
Bah! Let the galled jade wince, your withers are
unwrung. They have none of *your* money. The woes
of others are your *diversion.* The Silver Bill a foot-
ball in the Senate; Congressman Western Windy's
anti-tariff resolution; the monthly statement of the
National debt; the four per cent. loan; — you pass
them by with supreme contempt. If the country
were placed on its financial head tomorrow, kicking
its heels amid the clouds of bankruptcy, it would be
a matter of the most delightful indifference to you.
The pinnacle of your hopes, aspirations and desires
may be realized in that ecstatic moment, when, filled
to the chin at the hospitable hands of some charitable
housewife, you recline at ease on the sunny side of a
plank and contemplate life through the hazy, somno-
lent contentment of a full stomach, without a care to
oppress you!

Fortunately, or unfortunately, (as the case may be
considered by the reader) Benjamin Cleveland illus-
trated neither of these phases of impecuniosity as he
walked down Courtlandt Street.

True, he was moneyless, — and for the first time in
his life. But his was a voluntary exile into poverty,
and he had the stimulus of an object. There was
something to be attained; something to strive for; —
an object in life.

And a life without an object is death in masquerade.

One magical name was constantly in his mind. The name of the goal: — New Orleans.

What his sensations were as he walked toward the Jersey City Ferry would be hard to analyze. He felt somewhat sheepish and shame-faced. Every one passing seemed to take a personal interest- in him, and say, " Ah, we know you. We know what you are doing. We know you have no money. *You are a tramp !* " He could have sworn that such were their thoughts. To be sure it was all imagination. They were all doing exactly as he was — thinking of themselves. The world rarely pays any attention to you unless you tread on its toes. Plunge your finger into the ocean — withdraw it — look for the hole ! The ocean is the world — the hole yourself. Ben felt *queer.* The central figure of his thoughts was New Orleans. But the steps between New York and New Orleans were many, and he was but taking the initial one.

While dreaming of the future he suddenly came plump up against the present in the shape of the Jersey City Ferry toll house. Forgetting for the moment the empty character of his exchequer, he entered the gate and thrust his hand in his pocket for the requisite toll.

The pocket was empty !

Blushing at his forgetfulness, and stammering out something to the toll collector about having left all his change at home, Ben retreated from the gate and into the street again.

It was his first check. The first gate on his road. And to tell the truth he felt lost. Here was only two cents standing between himself and $20,000! Ridiculous! Nevertheless a very substantial fact.

For half an hour he loafed up and down the piers of the North River, wondering what he should do. Once it suggested itself to him to go back to his friends and acknowledge the attempt a failure. But he thrust the thought aside as cowardly. Go he would, though he had to swim to the opposite shore, or go up to Albany and walk around the river!

CHAPTER III.

PROFESSIONAL ADVICE.

WHILE Ben reflected upon the majesty and power of two cents, seated on a check post, he was approached by a seedy individual, who had been hovering in this vicinity eyeing him stealthily, for some time.

"Mister," said the stranger, "would you be kind enough to help a man a little. I'm broke, and I'm sick. I have a wife and four children in Philadelphia. I'm a shoemaker by trade, and if I could once get back home, I'd get work; and, on my word and honor I'll send you any money you let me have."

Ben thought of his own utter financial emptiness and smiled. The man thought he doubted his integrity, and hastily promised:

"I'll do it, so help me! I had all my money stolen from me by a man that I befriended, who said he had no place to stop. I've been trying for work for two weeks and a starving to death a doing of it. I'll—"

"Hold on," interrupted Ben, "I am sorry for you but I have not a single cent myself."

The man looked incredulous.

"It is a fact," continued Cleveland. "I want to go to New Orleans, and here I am stopped for want of two cents with which to cross this ferry."

"What, you broke with all them good clothes on!" exclaimed the shoemaker in astonishment.

Ben thought he was dressed very shabbily, having donned the oldest and coarsest suit he owned, but in the eyes of the dilapidated shoemaker he was, undoubtedly, arrayed like unto a lily of the field. He answered however:

"I tell you the actual truth, my friend. I have not one cent myself."

"Have you had any thing to eat? Are you hungry?" asked the shoemaker, thrusting his hand into a breast pocket and producing a package of cold victuals wrapped up in a dirty piece of old newspaper.

Ben looked surprised at this generosity on the part of one who a moment before had confessed himself as starving to death, but refrained from expressing his thoughts as he declined the proffered food.

"You've got along well for chuck, then," remarked the shoemaker, returning the package to his pocket.

Ben had a dim comprehension that "chuck" referred to food, and replied that he was not hungry, adding the information that he was only recently become "broke" and that it was the first time in his life such a predicament had overtaken him; whereupon the shoemaker looked at him with commiseration. Indeed he appeared so to sympathize with Ben that that young gentleman was touched, and said:

"I'm very sorry I have not something to give you, for I know how a man in your position must feel, hav ing a wife and four children at a distance and no money to reach them with." But this was not received graciously by the knight of St. Crispin, who looked at Ben suspiciously and gruffly said :

" What are you giving us ; — lumps ? "

Ben was at a loss for the meaning of "lumps " but answered pleasantly :

" I was speaking of your family ; your wife and four children in Philadelphia." This was said so honestly that the man's face cleared up in a moment, and he broke into a coarse laugh.

" Philadelphia be blowed ! This town's too fat to leave. Big free lunches. Five cent hang ups. Best town to codge in you ever struck ! Give you a reg'lar sit down here. Philadelphia you only get a back door hand out. Down there they allus think you're after the spoons and cutlery. Don't care a durn what you are after here. All of 'em after sumthin' themselves. All politicians here. Tell 'em you belongs to the Ward. Find out what ward you're in first. Give you big squares. Sometimes wealth — and clo'es. Give you a copper cent in Philadelphia, and make you go before a justice of the peace and swear you won't spend it for drink. *Here*, don't care a cuss what you spend it for. Philadelphia the lady of the house comes down to see you and ask questions. *Here*, the servant girl's boss ! If she's Irish, say you're a Fenian. If she's Dutch, tell her you've got a sauerkraut wife. If she's a nigger, just tell her you're hungry. Go striking in Philadelphia and they'll hand you over to the police. Strike a man here and he's *white !* Give him a stiff on some good trade. But

look out you don't get caught up.   I struck a man
this mornin' and give him that I was a blacksmith.
Thunder! What you suppose! He took me about
six blocks, up to where he lived over his own shop,
and give me a big sit down.   Then he took me down
to the shop and told me he'd give me work for the next
three months, and wanted me to go right to business!
I pulled off my coat and let on that I'd struck oil at
last, an' then, of a sudden, told him I'd a keyster
down at a hang up with a leather apron in it, an' I'd
have to go after it.   He wanted to lend me an apron,
but I told him I was so used to this one that I could
not work without it nohow.

"You see you must be careful who you strike.
But I s'pects you're a fresh one.   Now take my advice: unless there's big inducements taking you to
New Orleans, don't you leave this town.   You're well
dressed, an' you look well.   Why, with those togs on,
and that light over-Benny you can beat the restaur-
ants and lunches for the next twelve months!   Tramping aint what it used to be.   It's overdone.   There's
too many working at the business.   There's no money
in it.   You stay here."

Though Ben did not more than half understand
what the whilom shoemaker had been saying, he nevertheless realized that he was conversing with a professional parasite,— one of those social excrescences,
so many of which are to be found in all large citi
He thanked him, however, for the kind interest he
took in his welfare, but reiterated his determination
to go to New Orleans.

"Then go by boat.   Beat your way on a steamer.

Stow away, and when they're off once they can't land you except they run into Havana."

" But I want to go to St. Louis first," said Ben.

" St. Louis is a good town. You hear *me!* The soup season aint commenced yet. But they set boss free lunches!" And the professional rolled his eyes as he mentioned the delights of the Future Great City.

. " I'm much obliged to you for the information, I'm sure," replied Ben. " But what troubles me just at present is to cross this ferry."

" To cross the ferry ? "

" Yes."

" Poh ! That's the easiest thing in the world. Go give 'em a racket. Go to the wagon gate, I would. The box man's too busy to attend to you. Tell the man there you just had your pocket picked and must get over in time to catch the Elizabeth train. Tell him you'll pay him when you come back in the morning. Your clothes will carry you through." And the shoemaker smiled on Ben's wardrobe approvingly.

" Thanks for your advice ; but to be frank, I had rather not tell what is not so."

The eyes of the professional opened to their widest extent.

" Gosh ! Where'd you say you were a going ? New Orleans ! Well, mebbe you'll get there — mebbe not. See here, was that a stiff you was givin' me ? "

Ben replied that he did not fully comprehend what a " stiff " might be, but he assured his interlocutor that he was sincere relative to a due regard for the truth.

The shoemaker was evidently puzzled. He could not understand the moral that could prevent a man from attaining a convenience within the reach of a lie. But his astonishment was tinctured with a respect for a virtue he could not comprehend.

"It's all right, I s'pose," he remarked, "but it's *too* funny for me. You're the first man I ever met that wouldn't tell whatever suited him to get along easy. Why, look a here; you go up and tell that gate keeper you're bust, and want to go over. He'll laugh at you. Look on you with contempt. Go tell him you live in Newark, and have just had your pocket picked. He'll respect you, and treat you civilly, whether he believes you or not; ten to one he'll let you over. Lemme tell you somethin' as may be useful to you on your way. There's no premiums for truth, but there's an everlasting lot of chromos goes with good lies. Now if it's agin your conscience to gin the gate keeper a racket, the only other way I know for you to get over is to go up the street a piece and jump a wagon. Gin the driver a good talk, and get him to take you. So long, my friend. I wish you luck. The band's about to play over in the Bowery, an' if I aint on hand in time, some unprincipled vagabond will have my dress-circle seat with a lamp-post back. So long!" And shaking Ben by the hand, the shoemaker turned and disappeared up a neighboring thoroughfare.

Ignoring the professional's moral advice, our friend proceeded a short distance from the ferry, and meeting a jovial, round-faced Hibernian, driving a dray, told his desire to go over, and the impecunious position in which he was placed. The driver kindly gave him a lift, and the gate was safely passed. On the ferry, Ben answered the driver's numerous inquiries as explicitly as he thought proper, and quite an acquaintance was struck between them. When the boat had deposited them on the Jersey City side he dismounted, and after thanking the driver was about proceeding on his way, when the latter thrust out a dirty, toil soiled hand, and forced a quarter of a dollar on him. "It aint much, but it'll help yez get a mouthful to eat," and without waiting either protestations or thanks, the man put whip to his team and drove off.

CHAPTER IV.

OUR HERO MEETS HIS DESTINY.

"WELL, it *is* charity," said Ben to himself, "but it is acceptable for all that." He then strolled up the gaslit street,—for it had been dark for some little time — and repeatedly asked himself what would be the next move in the campaign he had undertaken.

The "prodigal" had spoken of riding ; how was it to be done ? Should he enter a train, take a seat and wait until the conductor put him off ? He knew that that manner of proceeding would gain him but a short ride. Perhaps he might tell the conductor a pathetic tale that would so work upon that individual's generosity that he would allow him to continue on the train. Alas, he knew the craft too well to attempt so futile an undertaking. Not that conductors are a hard-hearted class of persons, but their orders are strict, and permitting a free ride would subject them to a peremptory discharge. In fact Ben was lost. At a distance the simple matter of going from place to place looked easy enough of accomplishment, but now that he was brought face to face with the problem its solution became a difficult (indeed he was about thinking an impossible) task. What to do or where to go he knew not. For a time he gazed listlessly into the shop windows, and mechanically strolled along. If he could only meet a tramp, he thought, he would ask him how to proceed; and he kept a sharp lookout for one of the fraternity, but none presented themselves. It soon grew late, and the streets lonely. The pedestrians became fewer and fewer, and the shops, one by one, put up their shutters. Ben thought he had never felt so lonesome in all his life; and he was right. There is no situation in life more lonely, than to be alone in a great city at night fall. In the woods a man has Nature to listen to and commune with. On the prairies there are the stars and the night breeze for companions. But in a metropolis, a stranger among our fellow men, such a wretched, helpless feeling comes over the traveller that his loneliness seats itself, not only on his mind, but on his heart. This feeling was creeping with a dull, heavy tread upon Ben, and he had already commenced to anxiously question himself where he should pass the night that was now surrounding him, when his attention was suddenly aroused by a youthful voice, in a dark side street, close by, crying out:

" Let me alone! Let me alone, I say!" and then a gentle female voice entreating:

" Do not strike the boy, Arthur. Do not beat him. He did not mean to; I am sure he did not!"

"I'll teach you to pick a pocket, you young scoundrel!" exclaimed an angry man; and there followed a blow, and a cry of pain.

By this time Ben, who had accelerated his step, reached the scene of disturbance, and discovered by the dim light that crept from a street lamp, half a block away, a large man grasping a boy by the arm, and holding an uplifted cane, that a young lady was striving to prevent again descending upon the captive. The face of the latter being concealed by an old slouch hat jammed down over his eyes.

In Ben's nature was a strong love of justice. He had ever been a champion of the weak, and an injury inflicted by a strong arm on one incapable of resistance was an outrage on his own sensitiveness, that had involved him in many a rough-and-tumble while a boy at school and college. As the man shook off his fair companion's hand and the cane was about descending again on the shrinking person of the boy, he interposed his arm and caught the blow upon it.

"Don't strike the boy, sir. Please do not hit him. Even if he has done wrong a beating will not improve him." As he thus expostulated with the man he became conscious of a pair of great, glorious, grey eyes, that fairly glowed in the dark, looking gratefully upon him from out the folds of a snowy nubia, and a very melodious voice seconding his own entreaties, with:

"I'm sure you are mistaken, Arthur. This gentleman is right. Pray do not strike the boy again."

But Ben's observations reached no farther, for the man gave him a stinging blow across the face with the cane, exclaiming fiercely:

"Confound your impudence, who asked you to interfere!" The next moment the man lay at length in the gutter, having been sent there by a powerful and well directed blow with which, in the heat of the moment, Ben had resented the indignity received by him.

The next instant he repented such an act in the presence of a lady and turned to apologize, when a warning voice cried, " Look out! He is armed!" and he saw that his opponent had regained his feet and was drawing a weapon from his pocket. What the result might have been, had the man been allowed to use his revolver, is not difficult to surmise. A shot at such close quarters would probably have suddenly terminated Ben's tramp, had not the boy who gave the warning struck the man on the head with a stone before he had an opportunity to use the weapon he was uncovering. The blow was a severe one, and felled him senseless to the pavement.

" Come, come!" cried the boy, " Let us get away from here!"

But Ben would not leave his fallen enemy without ascertaining the extent of his injuries, and he immediately offered his assistance to the young lady, who now stood beside her senseless escort, wringing her hands, and vainly imploring him to arise. He had been only stunned, however, and as Ben stooped over him showed signs of returning consciousness. Attempting to rise to his feet, he found himself still too dazed from the effects of the blow, and would have fallen had not Cleveland supported him.

" I am very sorry this should have occurred, Miss, but really this gentleman is alone responsible for it," said Ben apologetically.

" Yes," she replied graciously. " No doubt you are right, sir. I do not think the boy intended any wrong, but — but Arthur was ill tempered on account of other matters, and — allowed his anger to vent itself on the first object it came across."

And Ben thought he noticed, that, though nervous from the excitement, she did not appear to evince much sympathy for her companion. The latter soon recovered his senses sufficiently to keep his feet, and supporting himself by the young lady's arm prepared to leave. As he was moving off he turned upon Ben and said, with a malevolent scowl : " I will remember you, sir."

" I trust, miss, you will pardon me for my rudeness," said our hero, addressing the young lady and ignoring her companion. " I am very sorry for what has occurred. Here is his pistol. I hope the next time he draws it, it will be in defence of a more manly action than striking one too small to defend himself." And he handed the revolver to the young lady, who received it with a simple " thank you, sir." Ben lifted his hat courteously, and the fair one returned a smile and an inclination of her head; and the three separated.

Our friend stood watching the retreating figures of the lady and her escort, until they were lost in the darkness, and then, instead of resuming his walk, he leaned against a neighboring wall, while his thoughts continued to follow the owner of the great, glorious, gray eyes in the nubia.

Unconscious of his surroundings, his mind basked in the light of the bewildering glances, and his ears danced to the music of the voice that had proceeded from out the folds of the snowy nubia. Ben had a large circle of young lady acquaintances, and, being a fellow of culture and good looks, was a favorite with the fair sex. Among them might have been numbered many attractive and *polished* misses, some of whom had treated our hero more than cordially. But for all he retained the same simple feeling of friendship, — and, nothing deeper. There was a latent feeling in the young man's composition that had never been touched until that evening. A wonderful change had now come over him. He felt that she of the nubia was a fragment (and a pretty large one) of his own existence. And it is singular, yet true, should he never again have set eyes upon her, there would have remained for life a tender memory in his heart that nothing could have displaced.

There is many a heart, going about this world today, with just such an uncompleted vision, locked up as a sacred secret within.

" Pshaw ! " he said to himself, " we probably will never meet again." At the same time there was a small voice, aiding and abetting a sanguine hope, which kept saying : " Yes you will, Ben. Depend upon it, you will, my boy ! "

Happening to look up from his musings, he discovered the cause of the recent encounter standing a few feet away, attentively observing him. The lad, finding his presence noticed, approached closer and said in a singularly soft, pleasant voice :

" I thank you ever so much. I chanced to run against that man in the dark, and he called me a

thief. I called him a liar. Then he struck me. I'm
no *thief!*"

" Do you know the man?" asked Ben.

There was considerable hesitancy in the boy's manner as he answered: " No — no — I don't know him.
But I *will*, if I see him again, and I won't forget that
he struck me, either."

" I wish you knew him," said Ben.

" Why?" asked the other in surprise.

Ben blushed all to himself in the dark, but, reasoning that it was " only a boy," boldly answered:

" I should like to know whom his lady companion
is."

"Oh! Is *that* it!" and the way he said it sounded
singular to Ben.   " Well, I suppose you live here and
will have a chance to find out."

" No, I do not live here.   I live in New York."

" Going home tonight?" inquired the lad.

" No," laughed Ben.   " I'm going to St. Louis before
I go home again."

" To St. Louis!   I declare!   There is where I'm
going myself."

" Perhaps we may travel together," suggested Ben,
laughing.

" No fear of that," replied the other.   " I guess my
way of travelling wouldn't suit you.   I go in a Pullman Palace box car," and the boy laughed merrily.

" A what car? "

" A Pullman Palace Box!" returned the boy.
" I'm going to beat my way."

At last, thought Ben, I see a way out of the
woods *!*

" Are you indeed ! That is identically the way I am going to travel. Do you think you can get to St. Louis ? "

" Get there ! " exclaimed the patron of the palace box disdainfully. " Get there ! Well, I should say, I have just made it from Boston here, and I made it from Montreal to Boston. I know all the ropes, now; — sure as you live, I do. And are you broke too ? "

" Yes," replied Cleveland ; " and that is not the worst of it. I never was broke before, and, to tell the truth, I'm a novice at beating my way, and do not know just how to do it."

" Why, so far as that goes, beating one's way is like any other kind of work. *It is work.* To be sure it's not quite so pleasant as *paying* your way, and you have to put up with a good bit, but if you have the nerve you may rest assured that you will get to your destination all right. As we are going the same way, suppose we go together ? "

" Agreed ! " said Ben, glad to have fallen in with some one posted in the vagabond life he was about entering upon.

" Then we're pards. Here's my hand on it ! " and Ben grasped a warm, soft hand in his and the compact was duly signed and sealed.

" Now, partner," said the boy, " as you say you are new to the business, let me have the direction of affairs until you get your hand in. We will have to stay here for tonight, because the yards and tracks are watched so close that it is next to impossible to jump a train going out of here. But to-morrow we will foot it down to Elizabeth, and make some side track below that town, and jump a train in the evening. To-morrow night, by this time, we can make Philadelphia. That will be a good time to jump some coal flats and get out on the Central road."

"You speak as though you had been over the route," said Ben in admiration of the practical manner in which his new acquaintance handled the subject. He felt a great relief in having found a companion who could tell him something about travelling in the new style, not at that time being aware of the fact that had he followed the railroad he could have picked up a score of free riders going in any direction his fancy may have desired.

The boy, however, denied having ever been over the road before.

" No, no," he said, " when you are on a tramp you learn to post yourself on these matters. It's easy done ; — see here! Here's the public and employee's time-tables of all the roads that come into New York City." And he showed Ben a pocket-full of railroad time-tables. " With these you can keep posted just how the trains run, where there are good jumping places, tanks, switches, and so on. All the bums carry them. They are their *war maps*. At the next convention the tramps ought to vote a set of thanks to the railroad companies for printing these things for them. But now let's go to bed. Have you any wealth ? "

" I have just twenty-five cents," replied Ben acknowledging the quarter given him by the teamster.

"Good enough. Keep your money for tobacco. Are you hungry?"

"No."

"All right then. We will get some breakfast before we start in the morning. Now let us go to bed. I've got the boss hangup. It's a shed in a lumber-yard. There's lots of nice clean boards in it. You must go quiet, or the watchman will see us getting in, though, after you get in the shed he never comes by that way. Come on."

Ben followed the boy to a lumber-yard, and having scaled a padlocked gate, they were about to make for the shed, which was dimly discernible in the distance, when the quick ear of the lad detected footsteps. Quietly he led Ben into a recess, made by projecting piles of lumber, and then the two crouched down, awaiting the appearance of the person approaching. That individual shortly came up in the shape of a man — and a very ragged one — as seen through the starlight. Behind him limped a comrade carrying a small bundle. They were outside of the fence, and halted when they arrived at the gate.

"Let's get in here, Billy," said the foremost in a low voice.

"Oh, thunder, Peters! My foot's too sore to climb that there fence, and if a dog got after us on the other side, I'd be gone up. Let's go to the Station-house and have a good night's rest."

"I tell you I aint agoing to the police station, like a slouch," replied he addressed as Peters.

"Oh, you're so durned high toned!" muttered 'Billy.' "There's as good men goes to the station as

you be, and if you get over into that yard somebody
may catch you and hand you over, and then you'd go
up for a vag for sixty days, mebbe. I wish we'd a
camped out in the country and not come in town to-
night."

"We *had* to come in to get some snipes. You said
you was a dying for a smoke. Come now, and shin
over." And 'Peters' commenced scaling the gate,
when Ben's companion called out:

"Get away from this yard, you scoundrels, or I'll
give you over!"

A sudden fall from the gate, was followed by a
hasty shuffling of feet, and the boy said to Ben:

"All right, now. We have got rid of them. This
is my hangup, for I discovered it, and I don't want
any more lodgers. Come on."

When they were safely stowed away on the planks
under the shed, Ben asked:

"Were those tramps?"

"Yes," replied the other; "peach-plucks, I s'pose.
The country's full of them."

"What are 'peach-plucks'?"

"Fellows that tramp up and down Delaware and
Jersey during the peach season. They get work at
from fifty cents to a dollar a day, picking peaches.
Sleep out on the ground and live on corn-dodgers and
sow-belly. It's a star time with the bums, and I suppose there's five thousand or more of them ramble
through the peach country. You see work aint
heavy and they can have all the peaches to eat they
want."

"But I should think that even at those small wages

they might earn enough to keep them until they found better employment," said Ben.

"They're not after employment; they're out for an airing, and only work two or three days at a time. After the peaches play out, lots of 'em strike off through the country for the Wisconsin hop yards, where men and women pick in the fields together, and dance all night. It is the life they like. Money's no object. Let us go to sleep so that we can get up early." And he lay down at full length on the boards as though they were a bed of down. Ben followed his example; but the strangeness of his new position kept him long awake, thinking thoughts that had never before visited his mind. Once he gave his companion a gentle push, and asked:

"Boy, what is your name?"

"Tommy."

"Tommy, what are 'snipes'?"

"Cigar butts!" and Tommy laughed a sleepy little laugh, and was soon thereafter snoring.

Then came the sweet angel Sleep, and wrapped his arms around city and woodland, palace and hovel, police station and lumber pile, and took his weary devotees off on a tour through dreamland.

About two o'clock in the morning, Ben awoke shivering with cold. The damp night air, warm enough in the early evening, had chilled and aroused him. His restlessness startled Tommy who enquired what the matter was.

"Ah, you were not tired enough to sleep sound." And then Tommy showed him how to make a blanket of his coat and vest, by covering up his head with the coat and rolling the other up on the breezy side of him, and in a few moments Ben felt himself quite warm, and again dozed off.

That trick of making a blanket out of his coat and covering up his head so as to retain all the heat of respiration was a valuable one that he often thereafter made use of.

CHAPTER V.

OUR HERO EATS THE BREAD OF CHARITY.

B RIGHT and early, on the following morning, our two tramps deserted the lumber yard, and having found a pump, both performed their morning ablutions; Ben feeling a trifle stiff in the neighborhood of the spots where his bed rubbed him the heaviest. But relying on Tommy's assertion that he would soon view a clean plank as a positive luxury, he made no complaints.

"And now for breakfast!" said Tom. "Then we will start."

Never before had this matter of breakfast appeared of such magnitude to Ben. It was as natural for him to eat breakfast of a morning as to exist. It is so with thousands of good people. And yet there are many persons in the world who are ofttimes compelled to look upon a matutinal meal as an unattainable luxury, and respect it accordingly.

Tommy's cheerful invitation was somewhat reassuring, however. The two walked on in silence until they were well out in the suburbs of the city, when the boy turning to Ben, said:

"This will do. Now you are hungry, I'll war-
rant."

He did not deny the soft impeachment. Indeed
his well regulated interior had clamored loudly the
previous evening at the enforced fast imposed upon
it, and was now sternly calling upon its provider to
do his duty, and his whole duty, like a man.

"Listen to me," instructed Tommy. "You are
young at cadjing and I will have to give you some
points."

Ben not only gave an attentive ear but he took a
good look at his companion in the broad daylight.
The boy might have been fourteen or fifteen years of
age; a round, plump little fellow, with a merry face,
and sparkling, hazel eyes shaded by long, black lashes.
There was something girlish in his cheek, it was so
round, and smooth, and rosy, without the slightest
sign of those capillary advantages that manhood's
prime was to decorate it with. An 'ungovernable
mass of curly black hair straggled from under a well
worn slouch hat that had bronzed beneath sun and
storm, and become limp and shapeless in its career of
pillow and basket. When Tommy spoke his voice
had a clear, silvery ring, quite pleasant to the ear;
and when he laughed he showed a dazzling set of
teeth. Such was Ben's new companion. He looked
as though he might be a good boy who would do many
a bad trick.

"Listen," he said. "We must get breakfast right
off. You take that side of the street, and I'll take
this. Go to the back doors and tell them any sort of
a tale that comes handy; only don't forget to say,

every time, that this is the first time you have ever
had to ask for such a thing in your life, and that you
scorn to accept it as a charity, but want to earn what
you eat, and you would like to saw wood enough for
your breakfast. But before you knock be sure you
look around and see that they use coal. We have no
time to fool away manufacturing firewood. Now go
on, and we will meet down at the corner of the next
block; the one that gets there first, to wait for the
other."

Of all forlorn mortals, Benjamin Cleveland felt at
that moment the most folorn. He could have charged
a battery, where there was no chance of coming back
alive, cheerfully. He could have ventured any desperate deed that required mere physical courage; but
to go into a house and beg for something to eat, — he
could not! His heart jumped to his throat with all
the nervous energy that attends physical fear in men
differently constituted from our hero. Gate after
gate was passed, he persuading and promising himself
that the next one should surely be entered. Once he
did stop with his hand on a latch, but chancing to look
up at the house he saw a little boy eyeing him from
an upper window, and retreated completely van-
quished. It required all his stubborness and constant
thoughts of New Orleans to prevent his giving up
the projected "tramp" there and then, and acknowledging himself a failure. What was $20,000 to such
humiliation!

But another course of reasoning came to his aid:
" You call it *pride*, Ben; but are mistaken. It's lack
of *nerve*, my boy," said this new logician. " There

is as much nerve required in facing humiliations as
there is in facing a battery. *More*, sometimes. *Physically* brave men are plentiful. It is *mental* bravery
that is lacking in you and thousands of others. To
be sure it is low. It is humiliating. It is *begging*.
You will be a beggar. But you have an object to at-
tain, and it can only be attained the one way. It is
either do it, or surrender ! ”

This sophistry at last wrought so upon him that
closing his eyes upon all surroundings, he made a
blind dash at a gate, and without allowing himself
time to think hurried around to the mansion’s back
door, at which he was actually knocking before he
fully understood himself, and without once remember-
ing Tommy’s injunction to be careful and satisfy himself that there was no obnoxious woodpile in the vicinity.

A man answered his knock, and all his courage immediately oozed out. If it had only been a woman,
he thought, it would have been different. But how
could he ask a man for something to eat! He could
not, and he did not, but stammering out some irrelevant inquiry about an imaginary Mr. Brown, he blushed
and looked decidedly sheepish. The man, eyeing
him suspiciously, replied that no Mr. Brown lived
there, or in that neighborhood, and shut the door in
his face.

Poor Ben made his way to the sidewalk feeling
smaller than ever in his life. Truly if the $20,000 is
to be earned at this price it will be dear enough ; and
he had not the heart to make another back door appeal, but walked to the appointed rendezvous, and
there awaited Tommy.

That young gentleman shortly appeared, smacking his lips, and looking as well fed and contented as possible.

"I had a splendid breakfast! Mutton chops, hot waffles, fried potatoes, scrambled eggs, coffee, — oh my eye, such coffee! Three cups of it! Oh!" and Tommy, his vocabulary unable to furnish him with adjectives to do full justice to the merits of the coffee, rolled his eyes instead, little knowing the misery his bill of fare was giving poor empty stomached Ben.

"What did you have, partner?"

Ben very truthfully remarked that he had had a light breakfast, indeed not much of anything to speak of.

"Then why don't you go into another house and keep agoing until you're full?" asked Tommy. "Go back where I was and tell them I sent you. There's lots left."

But this proposition was viewed unfavorably by Mr. Cleveland, who remarked that he was not *very* hungry, (which was false) and that he would purchase a nickel's worth of crackers, which would fill him to repletion.

" Do as you please," replied his companion, but I advise you not to spend your money foolishly. You can get all the chuck you want, by asking for it, and can save your money for newspapers and tobacco — and (reflectively) hair grease."

Ben persisted in the extravagance of a nickel's worth of crackers, however, and when he had eaten them, felt much better. He also purchased a dime's worth of tobacco, some of which he offered Tommy, who refused the weed.

The two now took to the railroad, and late in the afternoon made a water tank and side track below Elizabeth, where the time table "For employees only," informed them many trains would stop to water and pass, during the night.

On the walk down the track, Tommy had made numerous excursions to houses along the lines for "hand outs." He met with much success and nearly always returned with something. Sometimes with bread, sometimes bread and meat, and once a lot of soft rice pudding, carefully conveyed in his hat; all of which he shared with Ben, and when they had more than they needed, gave to other tramps whom they met. They passed several of these gentry on their way northeast. At such a meeting, all hands would squat on the rails and a long confab ensue. There were two questions always asked by those they met. One was, "How's 'times' where you fellows come from?" and the other, "How's grub on the road?", All of them professed to be in search of work; which, no doubt, the majority honestly were, but work is at present a very scarce article in the United States.

These tramps either preferred walking, or had been recently "bounced" from trains on which they were stealing rides. Hardly any took to the country roads, — save it might have been in the vicinity of a town, — much preferring the railroads, from which fact they have derived the sobriquet of "cross-tie sailors." Once while Ben was sitting on a pile of ties, awaiting Tommy's return from a foray into a neighboring farm house, he heard his name called, and looking in the direction of the house saw Tom vigorously beckoning

him. A plump, kind faced, motherly housewife gave
him a pleasant greeting, and on a bench he saw spread
an appetizing banquet of bread, butter, milk and apple sauce, to which his little friend was energetically
devoting himself. Ben needed no persuasion to follow his example; the good dame; meanwhile, standing by, and condoling with them.

"I have a son at sea, myself," said she, "and Heaven
watch over my dear boy! I know not when the fierce
winds may shipwreck him among strangers. God,
forbid, though. You, young men, should be thankful
that it is no worse. And don't forget to thank Him
who did it for extending his protecting hand to you."

This was all not quite so lucid as Greek to Ben,
who judiciously replied in monosylables, as he de-
voured the food. On leaving, their kind hostess presented them with a large package of bread and ham.

When they regained the track, Tommy explained
that he had given the good lady "quite a racket."
The "racket" proved to be a pathetic tale of shipwreck in which the two tramps had taken a prominent
part, having recently landed destitute in New York
City, from thence they were making their way on foot
to their homes in Baltimore. While Ben could not
indorse the moral laxity embraced in the "racket,"
he nevertheless admired the milk and apple sauce.
The bread and ham made them a hearty supper that
afternoon, when they had taken to the seclusion of a
small grove near the tank and side track. After their
repast, Ben was about to remove his boots; for his
feet were tired and badly chafed. Tommy advised
him not to, stating that it would be better to let his

feet "get used to it," and that they would "harden
quicker" by allowing his boots to remain on.   He took
them off, though, and both lay down for a nap to
strengthen them for the night's work.

They were soon asleep.   Our hero dreamed of New
Orleans and its glories.   Of bread and milk, a motherly woman and a gruff man.   Of gates that would
not open, pull them ever so hard ; and doors that he
battered his knuckles to pieces on without there being
a response.   But most he dreamed of a pair of great,
glorious, grey eyes, that, indeed, had occupied his reflections the major portion of the day.

If Tommy's face indicated the thoughts passing
through his mind, his dreams were far from pleasant.
He gritted his teeth, and clenched his hands, and
muttered hoarsely as he tossed about.   Gradually he
rolled over on to Ben's outstretched arm.   And the
arm unconsciously closed around him and drew him
to Ben's bosom, on which pillowing his head, the boy
slept soundly.

CHAPTER VI.

UNDER THE CYCLOPEAN EYE.

BEN had just knocked at a back door and a man was threatening to set the dogs on him if he did not take himself off, and he was in the midst of eloquent protest, that he was no tramp and was not doing this thing from necessity, when Tommy awoke him, and he started up with his protest but half uttered, to find the night air quite chilly, and countless stars in the coverlet of Earth winking and blinking at him in a most familiar manner.

"Get up," said Tommy. "It is ten o'clock! If you sleep that way much longer you will talk yourself to death."

"Have I been talking in my sleep?" he asked sitting up with a yawn.

"I should say so, indeed," replied Tom. "I've been listening to you for the past half an hour." He did not further state that during the half hour he had bent, like a timid girl, over Ben and kissed him on cheek and forehead — but not on the lips. But such was the fact.

"Come, it's ten o'clock and the freight is about due," said he.

"How do you know what time it is?"

"By my watch, of course. How else?"

"Have you a watch?" asked Ben, in surprise.

"To be sure. A splendid time piece. Been running these thousands of years, and never yet needed repairing. There it is," and he pointed to the Heavens.

"Where?"

"Why up there — the Big Dipper! You can tell time by the handle of it. Now you *have* learned something. Get up!"

Again on his feet he found himself quite stiff. It appeared to him as though all of his joints were soldered together.

"Oh you will soon get used to that," consolingly reflected Tommy. "Bump your back against a tree and that will shake you limber. Hi! Here she comes! Now for it! Hurry up!" And in the distance was seen the great Cyclopean eye of a locomotive, and the rumble of the approaching train filled the air.

"Hold on Tom! I can't get on my boots," exclaimed Ben, striving to force his swollen feet into them.

"We can't wait, Ben. Come on in your stockings. Carry your boots in your hand. Hurry up! Here she is!"

Thus urged he limped over the rough ground with his boots in his hand.

"Not this side," said Tommy. "Take the other side of the track; they'll see us here. Come, look sharp and get over before the headlight discovers us."

Ben hobbled over the track and both crouched down behind a pile of old rails on the opposite side from the tank. While cowering there the train drew up with a rush, and a roar, and a screeching of brakes, and stopped to fill its own tank.

Scarce had it come to a standstill when three figures glided like shadows from among the cars, and swiftly ran and hid behind the pile of rails where our friends were crouching. One of them observing them asked, in a hoarse whisper :

" Goin' to jump her ? "

" Yes," whispered Tom in reply. " What's the show ? "

" None at all," returned the other. " She's a loaded train. Every box locked. We've been making it on the drawheads from Newark. That's your only show."

Tom uttered an exclamation of disappointment.

" Ben, can you ride bumpers ? "

" I think so. What are they ? "

" Bumpers. Drawheads. The coupling between the cars. Here's three beats riding drawheads and they say it's our only show. If you think you can, we will try it."

Our hero answered that he had no experience in the business, but was willing to make the attempt.

" It's death, to fall," said Tommy ; and then the boy cogitated a moment, and whispered :

" It won't do. You couldn't do it. Not in your stocking feet anyway. We'll have to let this train go."

At this time the whistle sounded " off brakes," and

the engine wheels began to revolve. As the train got under headway, the three figures stealthily stole forth, and plunging between the cars, the long screeching, grinding chain of wheels, appear to roll over them and grind them out of existence.

Not so, however. As the train sped away, each of the three was dangling on that narrow, precarious, bumping, jerking little platform, made by the links and connecting drawheads of the cars. A most dangerous place truly, and many a tramp has left them for Eternity. A jolt! The foot slips! A yell! And all is over. The tramp is finished.

But Ben discovered before he reached New Orleans that the bumpers were not the most dangerous place about a train on which men attempted to steal rides. When no other opportunity offers, as in the case of a passenger train sometimes, the trucks beneath the cars are improved, where with a constant roar in their ears, a storm of dust and gravel in their faces, and a cramped position — like a contortionist in his box among the bottles — these knights of vagabondage cling on like squirrels.

Sometimes there is an extra heavy jolt, or a larger stone than usual strikes them on the head. In such cases the coroner's jury discover that the man was a tramp and came to his death by being run over by the cars. What would we do without coroner's juries?

Tommy watched the retreating train for some time, and then said to Ben:

"Never mind; better luck next time. I don't think you could have made it on the bumpers. Here's my knife. Cut your boots so that you can get them on. The lightning express will be along soon, and we can make fifty or sixty miles on it. If the express car has an open end, by thunder, we'll *jump the pilot!*"

" What did those men get off for ?'' asked Ben.

" Why," explained Tom, " when the train stops, they take to cover so that the train men will not see them."

" There were three making their way on that train."

" Hard telling," replied Tom. " There may have been a dozen; on the trucks, and bumpers, and hanging on the ladders ; besides some that may have forced an end gate and locked themselves in a box. When I was at Albany, there came in a train from the west and I heard the conductor boast that he'd made *one* trip without a deadhead. Well, Ben, when they came to open one of the cars that had wheat in it they found a man inside dead as a herring. He had forced the end gate and then nailed himself in, and I expect the dust or something smothered him before he could get it open for fresh air."

" That was a deadhead, sure enough. Did they find out who he was?" asked Ben.

" Bless you, no. What does any one care about a dead *tramp*. I was in hopes there'd be an empty on that train that we could have jumped, and made it clean through to Philadelphia. Now, we will have to give the Express a whirl.

Ben had scarce got his boots on, after cutting them considerably, when the express was heard thundering in the distance.

" Look alive now ! " cried Tom.   " Follow me close.
She hardly stops at all, — only just slacks up for that
crossing ahead."

Down rushed the express on another track from the
one occupied by the freight, and as it slacked its speed
near the travellers, they sprang from their hiding
place, and hugging tight to the side of the still moving train, ran along it toward the forward end.   One
look at the express car sufficed for Tom.

"No go !" he hurriedly whispered.   " There's a
door in the end.   Make for the pilot.   Quick!
Quick ! "

Expedition was necessary, for the air breaks had released their grip upon the wheels, and the train was
again assuming speed.

Tom rushed in front of the locomotive and with a
spring and a scramble, safely seated himself on the
platform immediately above and in the rear of the pilot ; or, as it is better known in schoolboy nomenclature, the " cow-catcher."

Ben was not so fortunate.   With a scantier knowledge of their construction and the art of boarding
them, his foot slipped from the inclined grating and
struck the fast retreating rail beneath.   Another instant and he would have been drawn down to death,
had not Tommy's hand grasped his collar and aided
him up.

" Thank you, Tommy," he said warmly, " I owe
you one."

" You may be able to pay me sometime.   Aint this
old peaches ! "   And Tommy gazed on the great broad
pathway of light in front, made by the Cyclopean eye
over head.

The novelty of his new position was exhilarating to Ben. There was a spice of danger about it, that made it enchanting.

What if the locomotive should jump the track! Or should be ditched! Or run into another train! Or strike some stray animal! It rocked and swayed to and fro like a ship at sea. He could hardly satisfy himself that this rattling, rickety, rocking, jumping, sliding, groaning iron horse was the same metallic animal that pulled those easy riding, luxurious coaches he had so often rode in. It appeared to him — novice in locomotive riding as he was — that every moment the steel shod steed was about to leave the track and take to the fields. Singular too, it was neither cold nor windy ; for nestling close against the iron boiler head both felt quite comfortable.

" Tommy," said Ben, " suppose we should catch up a horse ? "

· " Then we'd be a horse ahead," replied Tom. " I met a tramp who had taken a ride on a cow-catcher on the New York Central. He was bound for Buffalo. Well sir, they caught up a big pig, and landed it all unhurt, but terribly scared, right into the tramp's lap. He hung on to it, and when he got the bounce, he took the pig with him and sold it for enough to pay his fare to Buffalo."

" And bought a ticket out of his hog speculation ? " suggested Ben.

" Of course not. He went on a big spree, got broke again, and beat his way through."

Ben was about protesting against such a misappliance of the means good fortune had placed at the tramp's disposal, when the current of his thoughts was radically changed by a lump of coal striking him on the foot.

" Hello ! What's that ? " he exclaimed.

" Wait a moment and I'll see," said Tommy, rising and peering over the rim of the boiler. Scarce had his head appeared above it however, when he quickly dodged back, and another lump flew whizzing down the broad avenue of light,

" Just as I suspected," said he ; " they know we are here and the fireman is pegging coal at us to amuse himself."

"What will we do ? "

" Why, we can't do any thing, only wrap our coats over our heads and let him peg away. They can't bounce us until the train stops."

But the fireman soon tired of his sport, and only an occasional missile reminded the voyagers that their presence was known in the cab. Once, Ben in changing his position, arose to his feet and looked the Cyclopean eye square in the pupil. Tom hastily pulled him down ; but none too soon, for a shower of coal announced the indignation he had excited behind them.

He really enjoyed the ride and could scarce credit his senses when his companion informed him that they had come forty miles. It was agreed to leave the pi lot the moment the train slackened speed enough to permit their so doing, and Tommy thought that it would be impolitic to attempt to " jump " it again, as their presence was known. Therefore, when the train drew up on entering the depot at Trenton, our

voyagers jumped from their perch and were greeted
with a shower of coal and a volley of imprecations
by the irate fireman, both missiles passing them harm-
lessly.

As they turned to look at the long line of passenger coaches, now slowly drawing to a stop in the depot, Ben uttered a cry of surprise. Seated at an open
window he had seen the great, glorious, grey eyes,
and their owner. Beside her sat an elderly gentleman, while in a seat, immediately in their rear, was
his antagonist of the previous evening. His own surprise prevented him from noticing that Tommy's face
had grown ashy white, and while the boy's teeth were
clenched until his lips grew blue, his eyes glowed
with an unnatural fire. Cleveland was about to move
off toward the train, when Tommy caught him by the
arm.

" Where are you going ? " he asked, hotly.

" On that train, Tom ; I must, I must ! " answered
he, little appreciating what he was saying.

" Don't be a fool. What are you going to do on
that train without money ? "

Ben immediately recovered his senses, and looked
dejected.

" What's the matter with you, partner ? " asked
Tommy as he took him by the arm and the two turned
away. " What ails you ? "

" Tom," said Ben solemnly, " it may seem very
foolish to you, but I should like to know that young
lady, very much."

" What for ? "

" I — I don't really know ; but I should, indeed I
should ! " he repeated earnestly.

"Ben, I'll tell you something for your consolation,"
said the boy ; " they are going to St. Louis, too ! "

" Who ? " asked Ben, in surprise.

" That young woman with the grey eyes."

Ben looked his amazement :

" Tom," he at last said, " who are you ? "

" I'm myself," replied Tom. " There's no mystery
about me, partner. That party is going to St. Louis,
and I happened to overhear them say so in Jersey
City. Perhaps you may meet them there ; and," he
added in a lower tone that Ben did not hear, " perhaps *I* may."

CHAPTER VII.

THE PULLMAN BOX CAR.

WHILE loafing about the depot, waiting for another Philadelphia train, a string of empty
coal flats and gondolas drew slowly past on another
track. Tom's quick, practical and *professional* eye
immediately noticed them, and also the brand on the
cars telling the road they belonged to.

" Hurrah ! " said he, " we've made a close connec-
tion ! Come on ! " and in a short time Ben found
himself at the bottom of a black, dusty coal-smeared
gondola.

" Bully ! " exclaimed Tommy. " Here we are and
no one saw us get in, so if we keep quiet and lay low
we are not likely to be disturbed."

This prediction proved correct, for they travelled
the remainder of the night in the gondola without
being noticed. The train went slow, and stopped
often, switching frequently, but as they lay at the bottom of the car and there was no travelling over them
by employees, they were not interfered with. Singularly enough, Ben fell asleep while the train was in
motion, and slept well. The jolting of the gondola

became rather conducive to his slumbers, than otherwise.

In the grey of the dawn the two got down at a side track, in the city of Easton, Pennsylvania, covered with coal dust and as black as chimney sweeps.

" We are across the State of New Jersey, anyway," said Tommy.

" That's encouraging," returned Ben. " If I make as good time right through, I shall win my wager easily."

" What wager ? " asked Tommy.

Ben was momentarily confused, but answered that he had wagered with some friends that he could make St. Louis by the 22d of the month.

" Oh, that's easy enough done. Let us have a scrub up, and then get some chuck."

The " scrubbing up " proved a formidable operation. The coal dust seemed ground into their skins, and despite much rubbing under the spout of a pump, Ben differed materially in appearance from the young gentleman who had left New York city but a day before. Much of this was due to the rumpled and dirty condition of his clothes, which were all creased, and gave him the appearance of having been run through a mill of some sort.

The two travellers separated with the agreement to meet at the railway station in about an hour, and perfect plans for future operations. Ben was quite hungry. His long night's ride had given him a vigorous appetite that he felt would have to be appeased shortly. He also felt that the past forty-eight hours had wrought a great change in him. He was no longer himself, so to speak. A new man had been born within him. A callous, careless, independent man, that had not been in his possession before. He felt indifferent as to appearances, and the stares of strangers did not annoy him. He shuffled along with his hands in his pockets, and head down. He *slouched*. A marked contrast to his usual erect deportment. In fact, he was becoming (though he did not know it) a tramp. It still was humiliating to have to ask for something to eat, but nature overcame his objections, and he proceeded to the back door of a comfortable cottage. The door was open, and a rough-looking, dirty man was seated at a table eating his breakfast.

" Well? " said this individual, surveying Ben surlily.

" I beg your pardon ; but — but — I'd like to do something to earn a little breakfast, if — "

" That's enough ! " interrupted the man. " Go work for your living, and earn it, as I have to do. Be off now, and see that you don't take any thing that don't belong to you. You tramps should be arrested. The country's overrun and ruined with you. Why don't you give up your lazy life and go to honest work like the rest of us ? "

Poor Ben hastily left, and felt very bad about his reception. After a short time his mortification turned to anger, and he wished a score of times that he could have the dirty man all to himself in a quiet place for a short time. He moreover determined to get some breakfast if he had to visit every house in Easton. In fact the repulse, in a manner, did him good.

His next attempt was successful, and a hospitable

housewife, after shooing her children into the house
with her extended dress, gave him a very substantial
repast on the back door step. She was evidently accustomed to back door guests, and said but little and
asked no questions. They had ceased to be a novelty.

Thanking her in a gentlemanly manner, — something that called a look of surprise to the lady's kind
face — our hero made his way to the depot, with a
feeling of quiet rest in the region of his late hunger
that was highly satisfactory and worth all the humiliation in the world. Who should he there discover
seated on the depot steps, picking his teeth with a
splinter and hugging a small bundle under his arm,
but the dirty man that had refused him a breakfast.
He was half inclined to go up and reproach him for
his inhospitality; but thought better of the matter,
and was passing on with a frown, when the dirty man
looked up with a grin, and said:

" Get yer peck, pardy? "

" What? " said Ben, turning angrily upon him.

" Get your commissary filled? There, there. You
needn't be angry at me. There wasn't enough for
two — I swar there wasn't. I'd invited you in if
thur hed been."

" Why you confounded puppy, you are nothing but
a tramp yourself, then ! " exclaimed Ben in indignant
astonishment.

" Incourse," coolly replied the dirty man ; " I never
'lowed I wus any thing else." And he grinned again.

Ben felt that this grin was contagious, and as his
outraged sensibility would not permit him entering
into fellowship with his brother professional, he moved

away. Ultimately Tommy and he had a good laugh
over the fellow's cool impudence.

Tommy shortly made his appearance, having met
with his usual success, though he confessed to visiting six different houses before his appetite was appeased.

A freight train stood on a side track a short distance from the depot, and after a professional explor-
ation, the boy returned with the intelligence that it
numbered several "empties."

"It is a splendid chance," said he, enthusiastically.
" I asked one of the yardmen and he says the train is
made up for over the mountains. We might make
Pittsburg on it."

A few moments later the two were safely ensconced
in an empty car, having crawled through the window
in the end, all unobserved. Crouching down in a
corner they remained perfectly quiet, rarely speaking
even in a whisper, lest they should attract attention
from the outside. Several times footsteps were heard
passing, and their coming and going were matters of
the most intense anxiety to Ben, whose imagination
made every sound a conductor's approach and an accompanying discovery. At last the train started ;
backed up on another track ; switched around some
cars ; and then all remained quiet again for a few moments, until the engineer suddenly sounded " off
brakes " with his whistle, and the voyagers were congratulating themselves on a start, when a dark object
was hurled through the window, and following it,
three ragged men, one after another, plunged through,
headforemost ; much the same as the clown goes
through the baker's window, in the pantomime.

"Helloa! Blazes!" exclaimed the first to alight.
"All the berths taken?"

"Hush," said Tom, "or you will give us away."

"That's all right. We're solid now. The train's
in motion," said another; while the third stepped off
the "wind up" to a familiar jig, in testimony to his
utter indifference to noise.

Indeed the train being in motion the chances of
discovery were greatly diminished in the voyagers
favor.

"Where you travelling, boss?" asked he of the antique carpet-bag, which proved to be the dark object
that had first entered the window.

"St. Louis," answered Ben.

"St. Louis be blowed. I come from there three
months ago   The town's a good town, but its always
crowded. Better go South. Cold weather's coming
on before long,

> "And I sigh for the land,
> Where the orange blossoms bloom."

And he wound up by singing these lines in a rich
baritone voice.

"Where are you fellows going?" asked Tom.

"Cincinnati, sure's you breathe," answered one.

"An' then New Orleans an' the jetties! We're
the United States Special Commission for ascertaining the depth of water in the South West Pass, —
that's who we are!" said the terpsichorean artist;
and another series of jig steps emphasized this important announcement.

"Hello, young fellow," exclaimed the third man,
extending a nod of recognition to Tommy. "How
de do. Got this fur, hev ye?"

Tommy recognized a fellow traveller who had journeyed from Hartford to New Haven in a Pullman palace box car with him. He recounted what had happened to him since they last met, and in return his old companion told him he had been to Albany, taken a look at the Legislature, saw the political bummers gathered there and felt ashamed of their company, departed for Troy to attend a municipal election, got on a glorious spree, been locked up, had the freedom of the outskirts of the city granted him at the police court, " beat " his way to New York on a North River boat, and was now migrating South to save the expenses of an overcoat.

From the conversation that followed, Ben learned that one was a printer, another a carpenter, and the terpsichorean artist an iron and brass moulder by trade and a variety performer by profession. They had several times obtained work during the summer, but the love of a vagabond life was so strong within them, that job after job had been deserted for this roving. He also obtained a glimpse of a fact that became more palpable, the more he associated during his tramp, with this class of American gypsies. It was, that underlying the rambling propensities, — nay the very instigator of those propensities — was the vice of drunkenness. In their quieter moments expressions escaped the trio that demonstrated a hearty contempt for the life they were leading, and a haunting desire to return to the paths of honest industry, and the comforts of a settled home. But however strong this last feeling may have been, it was evidently overruled by the thirst after those hell-

born stimulants with which man is allowed to destroy
the peace and prosperity of his fellow man. As the
printer remarked to Ben :

"I tell you, boss, there's not a ragged coat on a
dirty back, or a pair of torn shoes on the bruised and
blistered feet of the thousands of tramps that are
rambling around the country like wild men, but
whiskey is the first cause of it ! "

"Then why don't they stop using it?" asked
Cleveland.

" Give it up ! " he exclaimed. " As well ask them
to give up life. So long as the cursed stuff is made,
so long will men drink it, and the government that
licenses and protects it are responsible for the vagabonds it makes.   They're holding conventions, and
wanting to know what the devil they're to do with
the tramps? Shut up the distilleries and in two years
there will be no tramps ! Many men can not give up
the use of liquor when left to themselves. It is not
a habit, it is a cur — ."

" Oh cheese your preaching ! Here — this killed
me father and I'll have revenge on it ! " and with a
savage laugh the moulder thrust a bottle into the
printer's hand.

The printer, who was a man of middle age, looked
at the liquor askance a moment, and addressed it as
follows :

" Oh, you father of all curses !   Murderer, thief,
ravisher ! Stealer of men's brains ! Caterer for the
gallows ! Feeder of the jails ! Soaked in the tears
of widows, mothers and orphans ! Iconoclast, breaking the images of all we love ! Defying God, and de-

facing his handiwork! Daubing blood on the face of humanity! Smearing crime on the garments of society! Barring the door to Heaven! Paving the way to Hell! Curse you! Curse you! Curse those that make you! Curse those in power that allow you to exist! Fragments of Hell hurled into Nineteenth Century! How I hate you! — *How I love you!*" and with trembling hand, and glittering eye, he drank deep of the bottle's contents.

The liquor was then passed around, but when it came to Ben he refused it. In that box car and from those homeless vagabonds he had learned a lesson that he promised himself should last him a lifetime. It was "Total abstinence." *Absolutely total:* — the only safeguard against the *disease* of drunkenness.

Singular enough his rough companions did not take his refusal to drink with them amiss. The moulder said: "It's the best thing you ever did in your life to let it alone," which the carpenter indorsed, by remarking: "If I'd done it years ago, I'd not be here now."

But the printer said — rather irrelevantly, and quite profanely:

"We're all going to Hell anyway! What's the odds so long's you're happy!"

After awhile the three tramps sat down in a corner of the car, and one of them producing a ragged pack of cards, (which same, he stated, with pardonable pride, had been in every state of the Union, and on nearly all the railroads) they were soon engaged in the mysteries of that ancient game, "cut-throat old-sledge," the stakes being a pull at the bottle.

Ben felt drowsy, and having had but little sleep the previous night, stretched himself at full length on the car floor and was soon lost in a sound slumber. The travellers having securely fastened the end gate shut with a nail (to prevent other tramps from imposing their presence among them, and also to repel the curiosity of train employees,) kept remarkably quiet whenever the train stopped, which it frequently did, and so rode along in safety.

CHAPTER VIII.

A BLOCK IN THE WAY.

B EN was awakened from a sound sleep of many
hours, by a rough thrust in the side.

" What's the matter, Hough ? " he exclaimed, his
scattered thoughts not having yet all returned from
dreamland.

" I'll ' how ' you, you scoundrel ! Get out of this !"
and another vigorous poke in the ribs with a barrel
stave followed.

This last attack thoroughly aroused our friend, who
awoke to find the car deserted by all save himself,
while at the end gate appeared the face of a burly
brakeman who was thus unceremoniously stirring him
up with a stave.

" What is the matter ? " asked Ben.

" Matter? The matter is that you'll get out of
this pretty lively, or I'll come in there and throw you
out ! " cried he of the stave.

" Come in and try it," laconically replied our traveller.

The conductor, who was standing outside, watching his deputy's performance, asked the latter if any
thing was the matter and if he needed help.

Now it so happened that the brakeman was what is
known, in the language of the road, as a "bouncer."
That is, he was a hybrid combining the qualities of a
brakeman and a bruiser, and was frequently called
into requisition by the conductor to take the dirty
work of ejecting tramps off of his hands. So he replied to his chief that he needed no assistance, but
would send him down a tramp in piecemeal in a few
moments. With this he plunged through the end
gate, intent on giving Ben a sound drubbing. But
he reckoned without his host. Ben was a stout, sin-
ewy, young fellow, and an excellent boxer, though
his muscles lacked hardness. As the "bouncer"
reached for his collar with one hand, while with the
other he aimed a blow at his face, Ben gave him a
trip accompanied by a stinging punch between the
eyes that sent him sprawling to the floor; and with a
knowledge of the work before him, brought his ad-
versary down with smart raps three times successively,
as the bully strove to regain his feet.

At this unexpected treatment the professional
" bouncer " called loudly for help, and his chief, sliding back a side door, sprang to the rescue, also armed
with a stave. When Ben, whose blood was now up,
turned to face his new assailant, the " bouncer " regained his feet and stave, and aiming a vicious blow
at Ben missed him, from the fact that the latter at
that moment, by accident, stepped aside, and the stave
brought the conductor a tremendous thwack on the side
of his head. This so startled and enraged the la ter,
that howling with pain and maddened with the blood
starting from a gashed cheek, he ignored Ben, and re-

turned the "bouncer" his blow with interest, and in a moment the two were engaged in a give and take pitch battle.

Our hero was on the point of vacating the car, but noticing that the conductor, who was a small man, was about to get the worst of it, he turned, and seizing the "bouncer" by the collar hurled him through the open door, and followed himself, intent on renewing the battle outside, when he suddenly found himself surrounded by the majesty of the law in the shape of a policeman. Two other guardians of the peace attracted to the scene by the noise of the encounter, seized the conductor and brakeman, and the trio were marched off, followed by half a score of rail-roaders ; the two damaged officials breathing fire and fury upon one another to the utter neglect of Ben. The officer in charge of our friend informed him that he was safely landed in the ancient town of Harrisburg, and that it was five o'clock.

Fortunately, as it ultimately proved, the police court was still in session, being engaged on special business. The prisoners were therefore immediately marched into the presence of a short, plethoric Milesian gentleman, who upheld the honors of the municipal bench.

No sooner did his eyes encounter the form of our friend than he called out:

"What! Here again, are yez! What did I tell yez the last time! Ye're here too often, that yez air. Do yez think the coort was made for your consumption? It's twinty dollars and costs, or sixty days in the lockup. Shut up! Every word out of yez will be sixty days more. What's the charges, officer?"

Poor Ben was dumbfounded. He was positive he had never met this vicious little magnate before in all his life, and did not know that the greeting he received was the august manner in which the blind goddess of the police court of Harrisburg struck terror into the hearts of those who had the misfortune to tread on the tail of her coat.

The preference of a hearing was given to the conductor and brakeman. Both had now secured legal assistance, and a charge of assault and battery was preferred by each against the other. Their cases were set for a future hearing, and both released on their own recognizance; when they immediately withdrew accompanied by their friends, entirely neglecting Ben, much to his gratification. All the officer who had arrested him could charge him with was being a vagrant caught in the vicinity of railroad property; which same is a serious enough petty offence along the line of the Central road.

The little judge asked him if he had any thing to say for himself, and immediately thereafter told him to " shut up!" He then went into a lengthy diatribe against tramps in general, and wound up by giving Ben sixty days in the workhouse.

Our traveller stood aghast! There was no provision in his wager about forcible detention, and he felt himself lost. Here then was an end to all his hopes and ambitions. From a tramp he was about to descend to the deeper degradation of a workhouse experience. The little justice must have noticed his consternation, for he smiled gleefully.

" Oye, that shuits yez *too well*, don't it?" he ex-

claimed. "Sixty days boord, lodgin' and washin' at
the ixpinse av the county! Egad sor, it ud be foin!
Chur foin, me lad, chur foin! Yez hid bate yer way
an hundrid moils for the loike ; so yez would! We'd
have all the thramps in the country to kape, so we
would, be gorra! Pater, is the walkin' good?" this
last to a policeman.

" Yes, your Honor," answered Peter.

" Thin furnish this gintleman wid a good map av
the county, and the coort will suspind sintince for *wan
hour!* Nixt!"

An officer accompanied our friend to the door of
the hall of justice, and bade him leave the city immediately; and the little judge shouted after him :

" Moind yez thramp, if yez air found in the city of
Horrisbug sixty minutes from the prisint momint, Oil
set yez chu studyin' geology wid a hammer for the
binefit of the city strates·for the remainder av the
year. Now moind!"

Ben was so overjoyed with his freedom that the terrible words of this terrible little man were music in
his ears. His first thought on regaining the street
was to get out of town. His next one was to get on
the railroad track and strike westward. He wondered
what could have become of Tommy, and sadly missed
his little companion.

To retrace our steps and account for his having been
left alone in the car will not necessitate much of a di-
gression. While Ben placidly slept the three tramps
continued their game of " old sledge " and their application to the bottle. They at last became so primed
with the evil spirits in the latter, as to awake bellig-

erent spirits of their own, and as the train drew into
Harrisburg were engaged in a loud wrangle that was
heard by employees in the yard, and they were conse-
quently routed out of the car, and Tommy along with
them. Ben, however, was overlooked, and his little
friend viewing it as a stroke of good fortune in the
sleeper's favor, thought to allow him to remain and
ride through so far as he could alone. But the train
had received orders to sidetrack in Harrisburg and
await instructions, and while on the side track, Ben's
snoring had attracted the attention of the conductor
with the results already known to the reader.

Taking to the track as his surest and safest road,
the sun was kissing earth good night, when he left
the city limits of Harrisburg behind him. He walked
on at a brisk pace until twilight gathered its dusky
arms about him and then found it necessary to go a
little slower, as he was continually stumbling against
the ties.

About three miles from the city he was met by
two voyagers going east. These gentlemen of the
foot path informed him that they were on their way
to Philadelphia, and had been " bounced " from a
freight train some six miles back. Neither appeared
to have any definite object in visiting Philadelphia,
and were probably travelling on general principles,
thinking they might as well be going there as any
where. Their intention was to make Harrisburg and
lodge in the police station; resuming their line of
march in the morning.

These tramps were quite kind in supplying Cleveland with information relative to his route. They

stated that the road was crowded with tramps, going in both directions, but the majority heading for the west. They also told him of several good " hang ups," in the way of barns and sheds, that with the eyes of experts they had noticed as they came along.

Ben lost no time in seeking a comfortable resting place and was soon asleep dreaming of two great, glorious, grey eyes that looked out sweetly upon him from the snowy folds of a nubia. Then, as he dreamed, the look in the grey eyes changed to one of sorrow, and they filled with tears. Anon a look of fright filled them, and the voice of the fair one called to him : " Save me Ben ! Save me !"

And Ben crying out " I will!" sprang to his feet, and found, by Tommy's time piece — the Dipper — that he had slept nearly five hours.

CHAPTER IX.

A GLIMPSE OF DEATH.

CLEVELAND hastened down the track in the
bright star light, and arrived at the tank referred to by the two tramps, just in time. For scarce
had he retreated into a clump of weeds, when the
freight train made its appearance and stopped for water.. Ben had now some experience in boarding trains,
and in a quiet, stealthy manner crept along ,the sides
of the cars, with a watchful eye and ear for train men.
At last he found one with an end window open. It
proved to be a box car loaded with lumber, with just
the nicest little place in the world for a man to stow
himself away in. The lumber was piled up to within
a few inches of the roof, but between the ends of the
planks and the end of the car was a space about three
feet wide, in which he hastened to lower himself with
a congratulatory chuckle.

By feeling the boards he discovered that the load
consisted of inch planks, of dressed lumber, for some
three feet from the car floor, after which followed two
inch planking. The ends of the top load of two inch
stuff projected a foot or more, like a verandah roof,

over the inch boards, and made him quite as cosy and
comfortable a little house as the heart of a tramp
could desire. What is more it was warm and clean,
and our traveller stretching himself on the floor of
his apartment, was soon sound asleep, with the song
of the wheels and the response of the ringing rails in
his ears for a lullaby.

Long he slept, and well; until wicked dreams came
to abuse his curtained sleep. First they intruded
upon him in the shape of great, glorious, grey eyes
and a nubia, and several moments of ecstasy were
passed in the company thereof. Indeed many men
can make love better asleep than they can awake, and
who of the sterner sex, when young and lusty in the
full vigor of brand new manhood, has not had those
luscious dreams, a counterpart of which it would be
impossible for reality to produce ! If there be him
who has not had them — he has our sympathy. Nature has withheld from him one of the choicest bon-
bons in her basket.

So Ben dreamed. He was with *her*. Her hand
was in his, her heart beating against his heart, her
warm breath on his cheek, her glowing breast heaving
in gentle undulations against his bosom. She murmured love, confidence and endearments. He talked
heroically, and felt the cup of his happiness full to
running over. But there came a change. Suddenly
a tall dark man came between them, and attempted to
separate the lovers. She clung about his neck and
prayed him to save her. But the dark man overpow-
ered him. He tore her from his arms and wound his
own with an iron grip about Ben's form. He strug-

gled to release himself.   His struggles were futile.
Closer and closer grew the embrace.   It seemed as
though it was crushing in his bones.   He could not
breathe with it.   It had assumed the coils of a gigantic serpent, and fold upon fold was wrapped around
his body and tightening upon it.   He writhed and
groaned in agony.   His breath came short and thick.
His head seemed a molten mass of fire, bursting
with the pressure.   His eyes started from their sockets.   Yet closer, still closer, the folds drew about
him, and the dark face of the man became the
hideous, gaping mouth of a serpent, that licked him
with its forked tongue, and whose hiss sounded
deafening in his ears, while its bright, devilish little eyes gloated on him with terrible intent.

With a yell of fear and agony he awoke!

His clothes were wringing with sweat, and the per-
spiration was pouring from his body.   All was dark,
— Egyptian darkness, — a fearful, appalling black!

And though awake, the iron folds still held him in
their terrible embrace.   Was he awake!   Was it real!
Was it not some horrible nightmare that still accompanied him!

What was this iron hand that clutched him?   What
these terrible coils about his person, squeezing life out
of him?   What this hot, close burning breath he
felt?

Arouse you Ben, arouse and pray!   Pray!   Pray
as you never prayed in your life before!   The gates
of Eternity are swinging ajar, and you are to have a
glimpse of DEATH.

One hand, partly released, he extended upward.

Horror! It struck against a solid wall of lumber that completely closed him in, and converted his chamber into a living tomb. But *there* was not death. No, no. That was but the *trap*. Death came surging down upon him in the shape of four thousand feet of lumber, moving slowly, noislessly, but oh, how fearful and sure, upon his devoted body, as the train toiled up a heavy grade. Already the mass had pinned him to the end of the car so that he could not move his body. It was crushing in his very ribs. He found it hard to breathe. His head was on fire. He yelled and shrieked for help. Prayed; entreated; supplicated. All in vain. The revolving wheels crunched out a dismal monody beneath him. Requiem for a dying soul. And afar off could be heard the groaning of the locomotive as it toiled up the steep mountain side.

Horrible fancies took possession of him. He thought himself dead and laughed deliriously. Then, in saner moments, he called upon his God to end his torture, and send a speedy death to his release. A release from the slow, lethargic, creeping monster, that was sucking up his life atom by atom; hair's breadth by hair's breadth. In those few awful moments the panorama of his life was unfolded, and the dead past resurrected, revealing itself more palpable to him than the living present. Worse than the tortures of the Inquisition, where weights were heaped upon the breast of a prostrate man, were now upon him. Shorter and shorter came his breath. He hated to die! He would not! He could not! Ha, ha! The great, dull, shapeless fiend that was crushing out his

existence seemed to laugh at him derisively. Blood
started from his nostrils ; water gushed from his eyes ;
and the fiend with one great yell closed a last clutch
upon his life, and he was released from his agony.

When Ben recovered consciousness he was lying on
the floor of the car, and a kind, rough face was bending over him. There was plenty of room about him.
The last yell of the fiend that was smothering him,
when he lost consciousness, was the whistle of the locomotive announcing that it had reached the summit
of the grade. In the descent on the other side, the
lumber had moved away from him as steadily as it had
before moved down upon him. Had the up grade
lasted but a short distance further, his tramp would
have been over forever. There was blood upon his
face as a reminder of the agony he had passed through,
and he felt weak, limp and lifeless, while the clear
sun light was streaming in upon him from the open
end gate.

"That was a pretty close call, my friend," said the
brakeman, who in going over the cars had chanced to
look in at the open window and noticed our friend
stretched lifeless upon the floor. Though it was nearly
an hour after he had received his squeeze, the man
readily understood the situation and the peril Ben had
passed through. "That was a pretty close call on
you."

"It was that," faintly responded Ben.

"I remember you," continued the man ; "you are
the tramp that whipped Joe Brown at Harrisburg yes-
terday. I don't approve of fighting, but I'm glad you
gave *him* a beating. He's the biggest bully on the

road, and takes a delight in thumping men smaller than himself. Where are you bound for ? St. Louis, hey. And you aint got no money ? No ? Well there are a great many travelling in your fix, nowadays, and our orders are very strict about putting them off the trains. But I'll break rules this time, and won't know that you're here."

Ben looked his gratitude, and pressed the man's hand.

" You can stay safely here now," he continued ; " for the road's pretty level for some miles yet. When we are to go up the mountains, I'll come back here, and show you another car that's filled with barrels, and you can get in at the end window and go safe to Alatoona."

" God bless you ! " said Ben fervently. " I feel very weak."

" Yes, I see you do," and a look of sympathy came over the great, rough, grimy face of the brakeman, and looked well there, although the face was badly mottled with coal dust and tobacco juice. " I see you do, partner. And it's agin rules bad, and they *are* strict, but when this crew changes at Alatoona, I'll give you a good word with the man that takes my place, and you may be able to make it to Pittsburg. There'll be down brakes in a minute, for a crossing, and I must go. So long." And his burly figure crawled through the window, and out on the roof of the car.

Ben had closed his eyes a moment, when they again opened to see the face of the brakeman, upside down at the end gate, he being extended flat on the roof of the car.

" I say, partner, that was pretty close, wasn't it ? "
Ben nodded.

" Was yer *prepared*, partner ? "

Ben looked his surprise.

" Did you know who shoved that there lumber back off of ye ? "

Our friend shook his head doubtfully.

"God did it, partner. You might say a word of thanks, if yer felt so inclined. So long." And the dirt-begrimed, tobacco-painted face disappeared.

CHAPTER X.

THE MARCH TO FORT DUQUESNE.

THE train man was as good as his word. Ere they climbed the mountains to the pretty town of Alatoona, that sits perched like a crow's nest, on the summit of the Alleghanies, he transferred Ben to another car. And when they reached Alatoona, and the train changed crews, he not only gave him into the care of another brakeman of the new crew, but, as the train would stop there half an hour, he took him to his own home and made him eat a substantial meal.

Daylight was fading out of the west when the train drew out of Alatoona. The car with the barrels in had been left, and our hero was now safely stowed in one loaded with pig iron that had been brought off of the Williamsburg branch. Darkness prevented the traveller from viewing the glorious mountain scenery, in the train's descent from the hills. The great Horse Shoe Bend, with its panoramic views of mountains, woodlands, and valleys; the old grade on the opposite mountains, where — in times of yore — they sailed canal boats over the hills on rails, and de-

posited them safely in their native elements on the
western slope, together with the many enchanting
scenes this road runs through, were all lost to him.
Nor did he see Johnstown, with its great Cambria
Iron and Steel Works, the largest in the world (and
a popular resort of hundreds of tramps who journey
that way and toast their sides among its many fires
and furnaces).   Nor could he view the noisy little
Conemaugh, that led the rail road along its bank to
the foot hills below.   We say Ben saw none of these,
for, in the first place it was night, and in the second,
his patron — the new brakeman — had shut him up
in the car, and told him to keep the doors and end
gates closed, both as a matter of protection from the
prying eyes of road officials, and to prevent a horde
of impecunious travellers — like Ben — from entering.   The last was by no means visionary advice,
for at nearly every station and side track the doors
and windows were tried by tramps, who had awaited
the shades of night to aid them in " jumping " a
train.

Ben, still somewhat weak from his recent adventure, yet feeling in a peaceful state of mind from the
assurance of his ride and the beneficial effect of the
hearty supper he had made at the home of the hospitable brakeman in Alatoona, dozed on the pig iron.
His bed was a hard one, to be sure ; but when one
side was dented so as to be no longer endured (which
occurred every little while) he turned over on another ; and by so revolving discovered the important
fact that a man is in possession of four sides with
which he may lie on the hardest of beds in compara-

tive comfort by judiciously using them in rotation.
That is continually turning from left to right or right
to left, as the case may be, so that when No. 1 is worn
out No. 4 will be fresh, and ready for use.

When they arrived in the outskirts of the city of
Pittsburg, the brakeman appeared at the end gate and
told Ben he had best disembark at East Liberty and
walk into the city, to avoid being seen by watchmen
at the lower yards.   Cleveland thanked him for the
ride, and, as the train slacked up, dismounted to find
himself in the suburbs of the Smoky City, in the grey
of the dawn.

"Good enough," said he, stretching himself, and
rubbing his stiffened limbs; "good enough.   Three
days gone and I have made over four hundred and
fifty miles.   If I can keep up this rate of travel I will
win my wager and have time to spare."

As he walked toward the heart of the city, he met
several knights of the foot path who had rolled out
of lumber yards and from about the furnaces of iron
mills.   These informed him that Pittsburg was considered an excellent tramp town by the fraternity.
Indeed the generous citizens had established a home
for them on Duquesne Way, where they were both
lodged and fed in gorgeous style.   But, he was told,
breakfast would be over before he could reach the
"home," and as the tramps did not dine until six P.
M., and guests were not allowed to remain in the *salon*
during the day time, our traveller reflected that it
would do him no good to visit the institution until
hospitalities opened.   As he still felt too weak for the
road, he resolved to spend the day in fasting and view-

ing the iron industries for which the city is famous.
He strolled around among these and chatting with the
hands was told that the good town's glory was departing from out its hands.   Years ago, before it became
a great iron mart, the city had been the most extensive shipping point in the *then* "Great West." Steamboats crowded one another at its levees, and the man-
ufacturers of the east were continually departing down
the Ohio, for the southern and western countries, in
vast quantities.   Then came the era of rail roads and
the rapid settlement of the far west, and Fort Duquesne, as a great shipping point, ceased to exist.
But when this industry was wrested from it, the brave
old town adopted another.   The transportation center
of vast coal fields and iron deposits, she soon became
a manufacturing hive, unequalled on the continent,
and for many years upheld the reputation of the
Birmingham of America.

But there came a change.

Capital ripped open the bowels of Mother Earth,
and stole the ores with which the good dame was pregnant, in other and newer localities, far away.   Iron
works shot up their tall chimnies all over the west;
at Cleveland, Columbus, Chicago, Joliet, Indianapolis,
Terra Haute, St. Louis and elsewhere.   As a consequence the good town found its second sceptre taken
away, and the grip it had held upon the Great West,
so long and well, Ben found had dwindled down to
its coal fleets, which, with the vast natural resources
of Pittsburg's water-ways, it is never likely to be
deprived of.   All this he heard, and much more.
He learned that the city had a magnificent debt —

that was a thing of beauty and apparently a joy forever. No one appeared to know just how much it was, but all agreed that it was ahead, per capita, of any other city in the Union — and this was a source of much honest pride. For though the city's commerce and manufactures might be stolen from it by western upstarts, they could not take its debt.

Ben discovered more real courtesy and kindness toward poverty in Pittsburg, than in any other town he visited during his tramp. The inhabitants were sociable, generous and unpretending.

While our friend was standing in the doorway of a mill, observing the men draw out the glowing, cherry-red bars from the rolls, and listening to the "bloom" snap and crackle, like a roll of musketry, in the jaws of the squeezer, he heard a little exclamation in a female voice. It was simply "Oh, my!" but it sent a thrill through every nerve in his body, for it was the voice of her he nightly met in his dreams. He dared not look up, but stood there, *feeling* her presence, and with the music of her voice ringing in his ears, waiting to hear her speak again.

But the "Oh, my!" was not repeated, as she of the grey, glorious eyes had only made the exclamation while passing in company with an elderly gentleman, and observing the glowing "bloom" pass into the squeezer. When Ben looked up, they were no where to be seen.

"Well," he muttered, "what is to be, will be. Tommy said they were going to St. Louis, and I may see her there. In my present condition it would do me but little good to meet her, anyway, I presume. I'm a tramp! Actually and professionally, a *tramp*, and I begin to look and feel like one. Should I lose my wager, I may adopt the business permanently," and he laughed not altogether well pleased with himself.

CHAPTER XI.

A MYSTERY.

"I TELL you, Nipper, if you will only give me half a chance I will make the matter all right. What do you get by pushing me so? The plain facts are that if you have me arrested, you get *nothing;* whereas if you let me alone I will do as I have promised, and you shall not only have the full value of the notes, but the bonus besides."

Ben listened intently for the answer. It was in the dusk of evening, and he was sauntering up from a view of one of the most picturesque bridges in the world — and the only one of its kind in the United States; there being only one duplicate in existence, and that in Europe. It is of iron and spans the Monongahela (Oh gloriously suggestive name! Whose delightfully realistic anatomy is so pregnant with remembrances of the liquid destruction our grandsires admired!) immediately at the point of land formed by the wedding of that stream with the Alleghany; the two thereafter journeying through life as one under the name of Ohio.

As Ben was turning the angle of a low wooden

98

A TIGHT SQUEEZE.

shed, the voices of persons in conversation struck upon
his ear, and the familiar tones of one of them caused
him to take to the shade of the building and play the
not very honorable part of eavesdropper. Charles
Lever, in that picturesque, but highly improbable
" Boy of Norcotes," allows the boy to state in a prig-
gish manner, that eavesdropping is reprehensible on
account of the impossibility of a gentleman using the
information so obtained, and immediately thereafter
causes the boy to tell all he overhears. Ben had not
read the book referred to, and did not feel ashamed
of himself. Nor having listened was there a dull,
dead feeling of lost self-respect that urged him to go
and throw himself into the river, and seek at its bottom oblivion offering a rest from remorse that this life
could never offer. Nothing of the sort. He listened
because he wanted to hear, and was glad of the opportunity. For the voice belonged to the man whom he
had had the encounter with in Jersey City, when he
first felt the influence of the grey eyes.

It was the tall dark escort, whom she had called
" Arthur," and he was talking to a thick-necked,
thick-shouldered, thick-faced, and — possibly — thick-
headed¹ individual, who appeared — if Ben could
judge from what passed,— to hold Arthur in no very
high repute.

" I tell you, Blackcoat," said the thick man, " I am
in need of the money, and the matter's run long
enough. You have been promising, and promising,
and promising, until I am tired of promises and want
something more substantial, or you " go up " so sure
as my name is Jonah! " And the namesake of the

ancient mariner who "beat" the whale out of forty days board and lodgings, brought one hand down on the other decisively.

"See here, Nipper," said Blackoat, "don't make a fool of yourself. It might afford you a high moral satisfaction to know that I was working for the state, but it would be no money in your pocket. Wait. Be patient. I can not compel her to marry me, and in another month, if she continues to refuse me, I will have the money any way — and the whole of it."

"Three hundred thousand dollars?" asked Jonah.

"Three hundred thousand dollars," replied Blackoat. "I do not ask you to believe me; go ask old Braster if such is not the will."

"Yes, yes, that's all right enough, but you are not keeping up to our agreement, Blackoat," replied Jonah. "You told me you'd marry and settle with me before August, and here it is September. It won't do. I'm getting no interest on my money," and this modern Jonah, whom Mr. Blackoat would have been so pleased to throw overboard and have a whale swallow, even if it did set wise theologians by the ears for the next three thousand years, stamped his foot.

"How much interest do you want?" asked the other.

"One thousand dollars a month, until paid, is little enough," answered Nipper.

"Oh, now the cat's out of the bag. That's what brought you on here, is it?" cried Blackoat. "I will not give it! I will not!"

"That settles it," replied Nipper quietly, and turning on his heel professed to be about to walk away, when the other grasped his arm.

" See here, Nipper," said he, in a tone of supplication, " be reasonable."

Nipper turned in a positive manner, and replied in
a positive manner that admitted no protests :

" Blackoat it's *forgery!* You pay me one thousand
dollars a month for the privilege of remaining out of
states prison. You will either agree to that, and give
me notes for it this very night, or I will sacrifice
twenty thousand dollars to see you get your just de-
serts. You know me."

Alas, Mr. Arthur Blackoat *did* know him, and knew
him only too well. He knew that this namesake of
the original whaler could sacrifice twenty thousand
dollars and still have many thousand left. He also
knew that he would do it if so inclined. Therefore
he remarked in a dejected voice :

" Nipper, it's the meanest piece of work I ever
heard of. You knew of the stipulations of that will,
and bought up those notes on speculation, and the
face value would well repay the investment. It's
the — "

" See here, no more of this, Blackoat," sternly interrupted the holder of the notes. " How I came by
the paper is my business. That I *do* hold them, and
in them have the power to send you to prison and ruin
your chances to get one cent of the three hundred
thousand dollars, is enough for you to know. Will
you do as I demand ? Answer yes or no ? "

" It's an outrage, but I'll have to submit," replied
Blackoat, angrily. " Come to the Monongahela House
and I will give you my notes for it," and Mr. Blackoat turned toward his hotel, with Mr. Nipper quietly
walking beside him.

Ben was about to leave the friendly shade that had hidden him, when a small, lithe figure sprang from the shed through an aperture made by a loosened board. This new party on the scene gazed earnestly after the two retreating men ; shook his clenched hand at them and muttered, " I'll have you yet ! I'll have you yet ! " Then turned and ran swiftly away in an opposite direction. Ben was so astonished that before he could call out, the flying form was lost in the dusk of the night.

It was Tommy.

As he slowly wended his steps down Duquesne Way to the great tramp resort he cogitated upon the evening's developments. And the result of his reflections was that there was a mystery connecting the owner of the glorious, grey eyes with Arthur Blackoat, who in turn was likewise connected with the thick man, Nipper, (who was evidently the latter's Jonah) and Blackoat in his turn was somehow connected with his little friend Tommy. But this was as far as he got. What the mystery was he could not surmise, and as he was not a very imaginative young fellow, he contented himself with the reflection that " Time tells all things," and hoped Time would not neglect its business in this instance.

" Well," said Ben, as he looked up at a somewhat pretentious three story brick building, fronting on the Alleghany river, " they have provided a pretty respectable-looking hotel for us people of the foot path, any way."

A short flight of stone steps led up to a broad hall way, that entered a spacious, well-lighted office.

Well dressed men were lounging about, and passing in and out, the same as at any other hotel.

" Indeed," thought our hero, " this *is* a new departure in tramping. How well they dress and how comfortable they appear to be." To make no mistake he stepped up to a group of three men lounging over an iron railing. Their tatterdemalion attire, and general air of conglomerate dirt and rags, denoted them to be the bona fide article.

" Recent arrivals, probably, who have not yet had time to recuperate under the beneficent influences of the 'home,'" thought he.

" Is this the Young Men's Home, the place where they take in strangers ? " he asked.

Yes. There was where they took in strangers. He had struck the right spot. He was to go right in and register at the office.

Ben entered without noticing that the three tatterdemalions ranged themselves on the sidewalk where they could get a good view of the interior, each having a face illumined by a broad grin of expectancy.

The office was a spacious, steam heated apartment. Ben boldly affixed the name of "B. Cleveland, New York City," to the register, and the polite clerk asked him if he had had supper. Replying in the negative, he was informed that supper was still in progress, and pointed out the dining hall. But as he turned his steps toward the designated door, the polite clerk called to him :

" One moment, if you please, sir. Have you any baggage ? "

" No sir," replied Ben in surprise.

"It is our invariable rule to ask a settlement in advance from those who have no baggage," said the polite clerk.

"Settlement!" exclaimed Ben growing red to the roots of his hair; "why I thought this was a charity!"

"Oh," replied the clerk, "you are in the wrong pew. Step around in the alley, and enter the first door to the right."

As Ben retreated his feelings were not improved by an audible titter indulged in by the loungers present.

(And right here permit us to parenthetically ask what it is that causes man to so enjoy the misery of his fellow man? Some one has discovered that the pinnacle of human happiness is based upon the miseries of others. Is it so? A drunken man reels, falls and breaks his nose. We laugh. A poor, poverty-stricken, hungry, ragged wretch is driven from a door. We laugh. A fellow mortal makes a mistake that causes him intense mortification and suffering. We laugh. What causes us to do all this laughing at the troubles of others?)

On the sidewalk Ben was met by the three bona fides, rubbing their hands in high glee.

"What did he tell you? What did he say? Did you gin him a racket? He won't take it, he won't. Ha, ha!" and the three were very merry, it afterwards appearing that the sending of fresh tramps into the hotel office to annoy the clerk, was an æsthetic diversion peculiarly acceptable to the trio.

The "entrance in the alley" proved to be quite a different affair. In a narrow, little landing, — highly perfumed with the odors of rum, tobacco, and dirt in general, — Ben's age, name, nativity, trade and condition of life were taken down in a big book by a man who occupied a small rough board office, and held communications with the outer world through a diminutive pigeon hole. Having furnished the desired information, our hero was presented with a meal ticket, and informed that the hospitalities of the " Home " were extended to him for three days, if he could not sooner find employment, after which he would have to provide for himself and pay the transient rates of five cents per meal and ten cents for lodging.

These preliminaries having been gone through with, he ascended a flight of narrow stairs, and was ushered into the greatest tramp resort in the United States, and probably the best patronized in the world.

CHAPTER XII.

THE GREAT TRAMP RENDEZVOUS.

A LARGE bare room, steam heated and furnished
with several long tables and benches, was already filled by nearly three hundred tramps. They
formed a motley crowd. Old and young, of numerous nationalities and every degree of raggedness and
trampdom were there. Young novices, just entering
upon this degraded life. Occasionals — working men
to-day, tramps to-morrow, and drunkards at all times.
Professionals, who preferred mendicancy to honest labor. Honest men, reduced by dire misfortunes to
this sore distress. Sick men, whose hold upon life
was waxing faint. Scorbutic men, bearing on their
face and persons the indelible marks that outraged
nature had branded them with, for life. Sad men,
who felt the degradation of their position. Bold,
callous men, for whom this world held no shame ; and
men whose deportment denoted that they had seen
better days, and could not forget them, were all gathered there in a heterogenous mass of rags, hunger,
dirt, and profanity.

No notice was taken of Ben's advent among them.

Indeed he was immediately swallowed up in the crowd, the members of which were variously engaged. Some paced up and down the floor, in lonely communion with their own thoughts. Some were seated by the wall patching their garments, and sewing up rents; some reading, others tossing coppers, and others asleep in all the hubbub and Babel of voices. Gathered in groups were men discussing the events of the day, or mapping out routes for future travel. What struck Ben as singular was the fact that there were very few *old* men present. Nearly all were young or in the vigor of manhood. He did not see but one or two old " war-horses " and they moodily held themselves aloof from the crowd. There was a hot, fetid air in the room, and his stomach sickened at this expression of the life he had adopted.

A word of explanation relative to this great tramp "home" will not be amiss. It was built by the contributions of generous citizens of Pittsburg as an asylum for the homeless wanderer. A place where he might rest and recuperate, while he sought employment. One would naturally suppose that those partaking of the charity would be grateful, but the tramps are not. A man with authority is continually employed in preserving the peace among them, and a more ungrateful, querulous, quarrelsome lot of misery it would be hard to conceive.

The building, which is a large one, is divided into two departments : — the " Hotel " and " Bum " sides of the house, as they are locally known. The " Bum " side consists of a single large hall, located in the rear, and separated entirely from the remainder of the

the house. The "pay" department, is a well arranged, well furnished, and well conducted hotel, principally patronized by permanent guests having occupations in the city. The proceeds of the " Hotel " are supposed to be devoted to the maintenance of the " Bum " department. "Bummers Hall" has an average nightly attendance of two hundred and fifty impecunious men every night in the year. Sometimes the number reaches to near four hundred. Statistics are kept of the attendance. Single men predominate, being above eighty per cent of those seeking the refuge. The nationalities represented stand in the following order as to numbers: Ireland, Germany, America and England; though all Europe has delegates in " Bummers Hall." It has been often questioned if the resort be not a detriment to the city, and an inducement for the fraternity to rendezvous there. But this is not good reasoning. The tramps would come whether the " Home " was there to receive them or no; and it is far better to have two hundred and fifty impecunious — and frequently lawless and reckless men — stowed safely away at night, than have them thrown loose upon the city. It is a difficult matter to make tramping a crime, for it would make poverty criminal. The suggestion that jails and work houses receive them is pernicious in the extreme. Reformatory institutions turn out finished law-breakers. They generally reform a man of what little good there may be in him when he enters them. The great · majority of tramps have not the *nerve* to commit a crime, though they had the inclination. They are a poor, weak, purposeless, cowardly set of vagabonds,

whose most henious offence consists in "jumping" a
train, or, perhaps, purloining some trifle of food.
They shrink from committing acts that will bring
them before that terror of terrors, a police court.
But a term in the state's prison or work house turns
out quite a different individual. As tramps they
still have latent hopes (however futile) of some
day recovering a membership in good society. As
prison graduates, this hope has left them, and they
look viciously upon life. As an evidence of this,
it will be found that three-quarters of the tramps
arrested for unlawful acts, are released convicts.

There is a great hue and cry raised every now and
then about "what shall we do with them?" Better,
if we turn our attentions to the *cause* that produces
the *effects*, and ask ourselves "what shall we do with
the system that makes them?"

Ben had scarcely time to look about and familiarize
himself with the place, when supper was announced.
It consisted of a tin dish of soup and a piece of bread,
and was served up on the long table in the center of
the room. The soup was of the "*bouillon*" order.
In it were sliced carrots, stewed potatoes, boiled po-
tato peelings, baked fish, chicken bones, salt mackerel,
cabbage, tomatoes, cheese, beef, beans, dried apples,
vegetable parings, and a few other articles. To the
imaginative mind it suggested the possibility of a
small grocery store having gone off on a drunk, and
got drowned in a cauldron of boiling water. A more
practical view of the matter was that it consisted of
the remnants of the "Hotel side," with the kitchen
dish water generously added, by way of a flavor.

Though Ben had fasted all day, he declined partaking of it, and sat toying with his iron spoon, and noticing the other guests. .They. had not his squeamishness. The greater portion of the three hundred were devoting a majesty of jaw bone to the work before them, highly edifying.

" The soup is extra to-night," remarked a veteran, as he fished up a mass that might have been fish, flesh or fowl.

" Excellent! " responded a neighbor ; "the best I've tasted since leaving the rotisseries in the Rue de Gumbo ! "

" I'll wait fur the toorkey wid the ister stuffin'," remarked another who had finished his pan.

" Yez'll have to wait, thin, for it's Friday, an' there's no toorkey. It'll be trout an' salmon, the day," returned a gentleman whose ragged sleeve had evidently enjoyed the soup in company with its owner.

" What part of the fowl do you prefer, sir ? " asked a polite tramp, tendering Ben a section of a mackerel's back.

" Let the gentleman alone. The venison he had for dinner did not agree with him," said a thin man, eyeing Ben's untasted soup longingly. Ben saw the soup and presented him the panful, which made the thin man an object of envy to all in that vicinity.

" Didn't I see you in Poverty Barn, in Cleveland ? " asked a fat, asthmatic tramp of Ben.

Our friend replied in the negative, when the asthmatic went into a glowing description of the magnificence of " Poverty Barn, in Cleveland."

" It's behind the police station, Sor. Bunks three

tier high, Sor. A plank set on edge for a pillow in each of them, Sor. A big stove that you can dry your clothes at, Sor. There's no knob on the inside of the door, Sor. So when you get in you can't get out, Sor. It's a good hangup, but no chuck, Sor. When you're in Cleveland don't fail to give it a call, Sor. It's deserving of patronage, Sor."

Ben assured him that Poverty Barn should have his custom if business took him to Cleveland.

" To hell mit Boverty Parn! I preaks my neck from vone of der punks down comma, von night. Youst, when you go mit Cleveland, youst try der iron vorks an' shleep in der varm sandt!" kindly advised a gentleman having a pronounced Teutonic accent.

With much similar conversation, the meal drew to a close, the pans were removed, and the long table turned, bottom-up, against the wall; so that having banqueted off of the top side they might sleep on the bottom. The benches were then arranged across the room, and an elderly gentleman in black, with a clerical stock about his neck, (who was irreverently greeted as " Old Blue Blazes ") entered at a side door, at the upper end of the hall, and proceeded to hold religious services. A more orderly and attentive congregation than the three hundred tramps composed, could not have been desired. This evening service was as much a part of the charity as the soup, and should it have been omitted they would have felt themselves defrauded. Cards, with the popular revival hymns of the day printed on them, were distributed through the crowd, and they lustily sang " Hold the Fort!" and " Pull for the Shore! "

The services concluded, preparations were made for retiring. Some of the fastidious (generally the most ragged) spread a newspaper on the floor to keep their clothes from getting soiled. Others contented themselves with scraping a place free from tobacco quids, and retired with their boots for a pillow.

There was one devotion peculiar to nearly all previous to closing their eyes. Everyone indulged in a good *scratch !* That great luxury that no unfeeling world could dispossess them of so long as they had their hands. And *such* scratching ! Such contortions in getting way round at their backs ; such grunts and sighs of satisfaction as both hands would be vigorously applied to opposite extremities ! And then the inventions of genius — rubbing the back against a table leg while employing the hands elsewhere ; and using a foot and both hands at the same time ! And such courtesies — one scratching the unreachable portion of another, and three and four scratching each other in a row ! Ben was about the only one present who did not scratch, and when a neighbor asked him to rub his back with the sole of his boot he could not refuse the kindness ; so while he did not scratch himself, he aided others. Let him awake at what hour of the night he might, there was scratching going forward in some parts of the hall. Before daybreak, however, he found it congenial to commence upon himself, and it took the closest application and industry of search and slaughter, during the leisure moments of two succeeding days, to prevent him from becoming a confirmed scratcher.

CHAPTER XIII.

INTRODUCES THE EVANGELIST.

THAT night was a memorable one for Ben. It is not often that a man lies down to sleep, in full sight and hearing of three hundred of his fellow mortals; not to mention three hundred with such peculiar characteristics as separate the genus tramp from the rest of God's creation.

Ben reclined on a hand and elbow, wide awake, listening to the various noises proceeding from the sleepers. Snores, grunts, exclamations, curses, prayer, laughter and writhing proceeded from the bodies laboring under Dame Nature's mild anæsthetic. While so listening, a tall, thin figure approached him. It was a pale, long-faced young man, who had an air of dilapidated gentility about him, that was in unison with his intelligent, but care-worn, face. Noticing Ben's wakefulness, he said:

"I see that you, like myself, cannot sleep. What a pen of human swine it is!" and he seated himself beside our friend.

"Which way are you travelling?" asked Ben.

"I go west in the morning. Which direction are you taking?"

"I am going to St. Louis," answered Cleveland.

"Very well, we will go together. That suits me. I thought it would be easiest to get on a coal fleet and go down the river with it, but I find the fleet is hung up here for want of water, and there is no telling when the river will raise. So we had best take the road for it," observed the stranger.

"Have you ever been to St. Louis?" inquired Ben.

"Oh, yes," replied he, "several times."

"Tramped it?"

"Tramped it."

"But," hesitatingly suggested Ben, "you appear to be a man of intelligence, I should think you could do better than leading the life of a tramp."

"Think nothing of the sort," responded the stranger. "A man in this world does just what he is fitted for. Habits, that I need not specify, have drifted me into this life, and I am becoming confirmed in it."

"But do you not struggle against it.

"Yes, I *do* struggle, but each struggle is weaker and weaker, and shorter and shorter. You appear to be above the average tramp, and as we are to travel together, I'll tell you some of my history without asking any of your own in return. I had a fair education and studied for the ministry. Until my mother died (and at mention of that sacred name of mother his voice softened) I had something to live for, some one to make proud of me. But on her death I was left alone in life, and though homage comes from all the world, it can not give a mother's praise. With a naturally unstable disposition I took to rambling, and I have been rambling ever since."

" And do you never try to settle down ; never attempt anything permanent ? " persisted Ben.

" Oh yes," returned the other with a laugh ; " I have been reporter, auctioneer, teamster, raftsman, railroader, clerk, stable-hand, and Evangelist ! "

" Evangelist ! " exclaimed Cleveland.

" Yes," replied he, and immediately the " tramp " presented itself ; " don't you know the racket. Lots of the boys made a stake at it last year. · It's the Moody business gave them a starter. First they evangelized themselves and then started out to evangelize others, with a weather eye out for financial matters."

Ben was horrified ! He had attended the Hippodrome meetings and been greatly impressed with the work of the revivalists, and had never connected a mercenary thought with them. This new development of using revivals for money making purposes grated harshly on his feelings, and so he expressed himself.

" And why not ? " asked the Evangelist. " People are willing to pay well for being led to the devil, why should they not pay to be started on the road to Heaven ? It is singular that men should honor money-making by all methods except the saving of their souls."

" But are the Evangelists engaged in money-making ? " asked Ben.

" To an extent — certainly. Why not ? It is dishonest ? Look-a-here, why don't you view this matter practically ? What's the use of giving it a fictitious reputation ? Is it dishonest ? No. Why

should not men make money in doing good as well as
in doing evil? Oh why should there be any attempt
to disguise the matter? There is where the mistake
is made, for it gives to good works a taint of decep-
tion. Do you for a moment suppose the world does
not see under the cloak of a '*call*' the greed of gain!
Why not be open and above board and say, ' *We* do
this good for money'? Is honesty a crime? Indeed
I half believe it is. When I started as an Evangelist, I fixed a fair remuneration for my services, and
demanded it the same as I would wages for any other
work. What was the result. I was called mercenary, and people said I not only laborized for the good
of my fellow man, but for the good of my pocket
also. I was fool enough to acknowledge it, and
shortly found my services no longer in demand. Naturally I changed my tactics. I no longer asked a
stipulated remuneration. I was not after money.
But quietly determined that money should be after
me. The result was I received more in contributions
than I ever could have obtained in wages. Do you
think people were not aware of my object just the
same, because I did not make a demand? Perhaps
you will learn, as you journey through life, that all
the world wears a mask, and though the mask may be
transparent, it is highly impolitic to ask its removal.
Humanity is an ostrich, with its head in a sand-
bank!"

"Did you make it pay?" asked Ben.

" Oh, yes, it paid well enough."

" Why did you not stick to it then?"

The brows of the dilapidated cynic contracted as
he responded:

" Because from a child I have been unable to stick
to anything. There is no permanency in me. I am
as shifting as running water. There, there; you
need not ask why I do not school myself to more
stable habits ; as I am, I *am;* and be it fault or misfortune, so it is."

Ben's mental eye looked upon his new acquaintance through a fog. He could not understand him.
At the same time the thought suggested itself to
him : " What a purposeless, objectless life! What
if my own should shape itself to such a result! " and
then the more encouraging reflection came to him :
" Better a tramp, with a New Orleans to be attained,
than a Ben Cleveland dozing life away on Smythe's
lawn."

His new acquaintance having relieved himself of
an over load of cynicism proved to be a pleasant con-
versationalist, and a well informed man. He was
apparently a harmless creature, placed on earth
to fill up one of the chinks in its great social structure.

The breakfast in the morning was a repetition of
the previous evening's supper, save that the soup had
fewer odds and ends in it. Though Ben had refused
the article the night before he found himself eating
heartily of it at the breakfast table, greatly to the disappointment of the thin man, who had purposely secured a seat next to him, with hopes based on his
good fortune at the supper table. Alas, they were
delusive ones. Ben cleaned out his pan, and felt sub-
stantially full.

In company with the Evangelist he made his way

to the city of Alleghany, on the opposite side of the river of that name, and there the two had a council of war. It was finally agreed that they should walk that day, and reach some point where a train could be boarded during the evening. Accordingly they followed the track that' borders the Ohio, until within an hour of sunset, when they found themselves near the town of Economy; a settlement of industrious Germans who are trying so to live that the transition from life to death will be hardly noticeable, save that it causes the reflection that for all intents and purposes they might as well have been born dead. It is a communal settlement, and propagation is unknown. By strict frugality, industry and the natural growth of wealth much money has been amassed, and the riches undoubtedly give them all the enjoyment of possession. One of these days when the last Economist shall have departed for Eternity, with his shekel done up in a napkin, there will be a delightful hubbub over the ownership of the thousands they have accumulated.

Before reaching the settlement our travellers were met by a lone tramp, on his way to New York City, for the purpose of viewing the abutments of the East River bridge. He had heard and read so much about that structure, while summering in the vicinity of St. Paul, that his curiosity was aroused, and he thought to have a look at it.

"I have not come from Minnesota direct," he explained; "I went to St. Louis to see the bridge Eads built so as I could compare the two. I takes a great interest in public works, and more 'specially engi-

neering. Sometimes I think I'd a made a good bridge
builder myself, but I served my time in a bakery, and
never had no inclination for bread, 'cept to eat it."
He might further have stated that being a gentleman
of impecunious leisure, and time not being money
with him, he had all the advantages necessary for indulging his penchant for investigating public works.

"You're near Economy now," he continued, "and
you can stop over night with the 'brothers.' I'll tell
you how you can do it. Old 'brother' Rapp will
meet you and he'll say 'no.' Then you just ask him
to give you a few matches, and when he asks what for,
say it's to build a fire and cook you something to eat
and sleep by, and you'll see how quick he'll ask you
to come in and stop. So long." And the tourist
again resumed his way toward the East River bridge.
Ben and his comrade had no intention of remaining
over night in Economy, however. They took supper
there though, being hospitably received and treated
to plenty of fresh coarse bread, cheese and smoked
sausage, the latter so hard that it would have made a
dent in an oak plank. Politely thanking their enter-
tainers ·they resumed the track in the balmy dusk of
evening, listening to Nature's vesper hymn.

Along the roadway, and from swamp and pasture
and woodland, came the chorus of a million throats.
The deep base of some old patriarchal serenader
heightened the treble of the noisy newts. Afar off
the tinkle of a cow bell floated softly over the hills;
the rustling of dried leaves; the snapping of a fallen
bough : the owl's whoop from out his hermit dell;
the beetle's never changing drone ; the call of katy-

did, and the mournful notes of the whip-poor-will, all
mingled in the evening service ; and the heart of Ben
stopped to listen, and all the sophistry, cynicism and
doubtings that this world possesses, could not at that
moment have prevented him from thinking that this
life is not the be-all and the end-all, here ; but that
far, far beyond the star lit girdle of earth there is
another, a better, and a purer one.

CHAPTER XIV.

AN UNCOMFORTABLE NIGHT.

THE two travellers boarded a western bound freight train at Brighton. There being no accessible box car, they were compelled to content themselves with a seat on the rear steps of the caboose, where they were discovered and incontinently "bounced" after being carried some twenty miles. Ben thought this ejectment finished their ride on that train, but the Evangelist—whose name was Horton —corrected him. Creeping along in the shadow of the train until it started, they again seated themselves on the steps. This time they made but ten miles, before they were discovered, when some strong adjectives were used, and some hard names called, and they were warned if caught on the train again they would be dealt with in a most summary manner.

"Wait for another train!" exclaimed the Evangelist. "Certainly not—why we have only been bounced *twice!*"

He instructed Ben to crouch under the cars at the centre of the train, and when it started walk with it, so long as he could keep up. When he found the rate

of speed getting to much for him, he was to mount a
ladder, but not put in appearance on the roof until
positive that the crew was not around.

The crew of a freight train consists of the fireman
and engineer, who remain in the locomotive's cab ; a
conductor who, while the train is in motion, generally remains in his caboose, and two brakeman — front
and rear — supposed to remain on top, but who, after
the train has started, usually betake themselves to the
engine-cab and caboose respectively. On the night
runs all carry lanterns, and through them their approach is easily discernible by the sly tramp. It will
now be understood why Ben was to delay mounting
to the top.

Having clung to the ladder for some time he slowly
raised his head above the roof and surveyed the situation. Not a light appeared in sight, but on the next
car he saw the dark outlines of a man, and heard the
Evangelist croning to himself a revival hymn. He
mounted to the roof, and both men sat down immediately over their respective ladders, ready to go down
them on the slightest provocation. Much after the
fashion of prairie-dogs, sitting at the mouth of their
holes, prepared at the faintest disturbance to show a
clean pair of heels and faint whisk of a tail. Several times during the ensuing hour the light of the
front brakeman appeared as that individual attended
to easing the train down grades. And each time our
two travellers suddenly disappear ; reappearing again
when the coast was clear. Having gone about sixteen miles, the train side tracked to allow an eastern-
bound express to pass. Ben and his companion

crouched under the cars until they again started, when the ladders were resumed and ultimately the roof.

This method of travelling seemed quite pleasant to him and he was begining to rest more at ease, and recline on his back, when a note of warning from the Evangelist aroused him, and glancing along the train he perceived lights approaching from both directions. The tramps immediately disappeared in the darkness, while the conductor and front brakeman met on the identical car to which our friend Ben was clinging. After some instructions had been given the brakeman, the political disquietudes of the day became a topic of conversation, and so interested did they become, that placing their lanterns on the roof they sat down themselves, to the intense disgust of our friend, who dared not elevate his head. Unfortunately for him the train was a through freight and had just entered on one of the longest runs of the division. The perch that had been comfortable enough for a short occupancy, soon became quite unendurable with the continued jolting of the car. His feet grew stiff and and his hands sore. Besides he had to cling close to the ladder in constant terror lest the timbers of the bridges they frequently crossed should sweep him off. To add to his misery both of the train men were great consumers of tobacco, and facing Ben's ladder they poured upon his devoted head a torrent of tobacco juice. Moments grew to the dignity of hours, minutes to ages. Never had he been so thoroughly disgusted with politics. He wished he belonged to a despotism where the discussion of them was punish-

able with death. Not only dared he not elevate his
head, but he was afraid to turn his face skywards at
all, lest he receive in the eyes and mouth a charge of
the amber juice that was being so liberally bestowed
upon him.

Our hero was certainly in an unenviable position.
If he ascended to the roof and gave himself up, the
conductor had threatened in case he was again caught ·
on the train to hand him over to the authorities the
first stop that was made; a procedure that, under the
vagrant laws would insure him ninety days in the
work house; enough to totally wreck his expectations.
On the other hand if he fell to the ground he was
sure to be either killed or badly mangled. In this
sad predicament his over-strained feelings found vent
in a groan.

Railroad men, as a class, are superstitious. There
are spots along each crews' route that are vested with
supernatural properties. We knew a practical man
of good common sense, an engineer, who solemnly
avers that on crossing a certain bridge at midnight, a
large white dog always springs across the track immediately his engine leaves the bridge. Another
man, a brakeman, would have deserted his train
sooner than omit changing his lantern three times,
from his right hand into his left, the first time he
walked the train. Whatever it is in the human fab-
rication that yearns after the incomprehensible we
know not ; but that such a force is established there
is verified by the scores of different religious beliefs;
— founded on faith or fancy — as you please.

The Administration was receiving a hearty endorsement from the conductor when Ben's groan struck on his ear. A sudden silence ensued. The conductor looked at the brakeman, and the brakeman looked at the conductor. Neither spoke. Another smothered groan came floating from out the surrounding darkness. The conductor was suddenly reminded that his way bills needed overhauling and the brakeman discovered that his presence was needed at the front of the train. Ben was left master of the situation, though unaware of the influence his groans had had in placing him there. He dragged his stiffened limbs to the top of the car, and indulged in a luxurious rub of his bespattered countenance. Presently he was joined by the Evangelist and the two recounted their experiences.

By constant watchfulness and much dodging down the ladders, they retained possession of the train during the night, and the first glimpses of the morning sun found them at Columbus ; having made over one hundred and twenty miles on the train Ben had thought it impossible to ride. Stiff, sore, tired and sleepy, but in possession of the satisfaction of having taken a long step on their journey, our friends dismounted and took a look around them. While they still stood by the train the conductor passed. He gave them one look of astonishment, and with the remark, " Well, I'll be blowed ! " went on his way.

As they stood staring about them, not knowing just what to do or where to turn their steps, a man approached, ringing an old cow bell.

" Just come in on the train, gentlemen ? " asked this individual with a polite bow and monkey-like grin.

The travellers replied in the affirmative.

"Wish to put up at a hotel? Right this way. First class house. Hotel de Log! On the European plan. Patronized by the elite. Table spread with all the delicacies of the season, and the best the market affords. My clerk was out to a ball last night, and I have to attend to the trains myself this morning. Any baggage? I'll send the porter after it. Just follow me. Breakfast is ready. You are just in time. Right this way, gentlemen. Allow me to carry your coat, sir." This last to Ben, who immediately professed to be competent to carry it himself.

"Very well," replied he of the cow bell; "come right along. You gentlemen also"; to two terrible looking tramps, that it was afterwards discovered had been on the train all the way from Pittsburg, riding bumpers and trucks.

Curiosity caused the travellers to follow the proprietor of Hotel de Log. He led them some distance down the track, and then struck across an open field to a piece of scrub timber, traversed by a brook. A short walk in this patch of woodland revealed the hotel.

A giant sycamore had bowed its aged head to some western tornado, and lay at length upon the ground, parallel with the brook, and about a rod from its brawling waters. Along the brook side of the tree were stretched, upon beds of boughs and leaves a dozen or more men, while two others stirred up the embers of a fire, near them. There were countless empty tin cans — fire scorched and battered — empty bottles of every degree of gentility, from the aristocratic, thick bellied champagne bottle, down to the plebeian blue glass pop, and an iron pot or two, while rags, bones, and scraps of cold victuals, littered the ground; and in the log stuck a piece of broken looking-glass with a fragment of horn comb behind it.

"Gentlemen," said their guide with a courteous wave of the cow bell, "allow me; *The Hotel de Log!* Make yourselves to home."

CHAPTER XV.

THE HOTEL DE LOG.

BEN and the Evangelist broke out in a roar of laughter, that caused one of the sleepers to awake and murmur a protest, and the proprietor of the " Hotel " to request them to suppress their hilarity lest they disturb some of the sleepers on the ground floor.

So our travellers bottled up their mirth and proceeded to make themselves at home, by taking a sleep that their exhausted natures loudly demanded. Having secured apartments near the fire, they scraped away such articles as encumbered the ground, and gathering together some leaves and branches for beds, were soon lost in a sound slumber.

The proprietor of the Hotel de Log was quite a character. He was a professional tramp and journeyman painter, who, being of a sociable turn of mind, had found congenial pastime in establishing and maintaining this popular resort. Originally he had camped on the spot alone, lame with a foot sore from the effects of travel. Passing tramps had been attracted to his camp fire, and in their stories of the foot path

and tales of adventures he had found the true pleasure that his nature craved. From tramp to tramp,
along the line of track, the word had passed where
good camping ground was to be found, and the Hotel
de Log never lacked guests. Hotel keeping became
a mania with the painter-tramp. He secured an old
cow bell and regularly visited all freight trains — those
being the vehicles generally patronized by his cus-
tomers — and invited members of the fraternity who
were intending to stop off down to his mansion on
the sunny side of the grey sycamore. He was a harm
less, good-natured little fellow, and liked by the respectable community residing in the vicinity ; for, to
an extent, he controlled the disorderly vagabond el-
ement that gathered about him. The citizens gave
him such scraps of food as they could spare, and his
boarders went out on " cadjing " pilgrimages, and returned well ladened. He was generous to a fault, and
had a kind, gentle hand for the wounded and afflicted
among his guests. The one great luxury of his life,
was the occasional indulgence in a quiet, solemn drunk,
during which he would sit nodding by the brook, and
holding pleasant converse with its laughing waters.

Who knows but the little man was filling the very
spot the Creator had moulded him for. If nothing is
made in vain, why should this little painter-tramp
have been ?

Heaven only knows where he now is. But it is
safe to venture the suggestion that if his cow bell is
rusting in the grass grown court yard of his hotel,
and the thrush sings undisturbed upon its walls of
sycamore, there are other bells in distant lands that

will welcome the poor little painter to a mansion paved with gold and glittering with precious stones. A mansion like his quaint Hotel de Log — not made by human hands.

Better, perhaps, apply for admission at the gates of that Great Hostelry, bearing with you the odor of kind deeds and the sanctity of a generous heart, than with all the pretentions of a successful life and most respectable burial, supplemented by a shaft of marble that shall hand your virtues to posterity in as cold and useless a shape as they existed while you were alive.

When Ben awoke the sun had passed meridian. The Evangelist still slept, and around the fire lounged two tramps with wounds upon their legs caused by unattended bruises received in boarding trains. The rest of the guests had flown.

Ben felt much refreshed by his slumber. One of the invalids asked for tobacco and he gave them both a generous supply. In return they spread before him the contents of the larder, consisting of bread, newly dug potatoes, roasting ears, and a jug of cider. The proprietor, he was informed, had departed early in the forenoon to attend a neighboring carpet beating, to which he had been invited. When the Evangelist awoke he also partook of like fare. At his suggestion, Ben boiled some water in an iron pot, and with a wash tub — improvised out of half a barrel — they washed their undergarments by the brook, and spread them in the sun to dry.

One of the invalids suggested if they were "*crumbie*" they had best give their clothes a " dry wash," and further explained that a dry wash consisted in spreading their garments over a village of ant hills, and allowing those useful little scavengers to go through them and carry off the parasites, both full grown and in protoplasm. Fortunately the " dry wash " had not yet become a necessity with either.

Being informed that a water tank, conveniently situated for "jumping " trains, was located some seven miles to the west, our two travellers left the Hotel de Log late in the afternoon — before the proprietor returned — and started for it.

The night that followed was an active and eventful one. The two were repeatedly put off of trains, and after having tried bumpers, pilots, ladders and roofs — during which they managed to travel some forty miles — they at last, about midnight, seated themselves upon the front platform of the lightning express baggage car, and made fifty miles without a stop. But, unfortunately, when they attempted to renew their place, the train side tracked, and they were discovered. An exciting chase between the tramps and several road officials followed, but eluding their pursuers, and convinced that it was impracticable to board a train at that depot, they took to the road and walked several miles until they came to an inviting haystack, when both lay down and slept.

Ben had now passed through the states of New Jersey, Pennsylvania and Ohio, and was on the border of Indiana. He had travelled over seven hundred miles in six days, and St. Louis was within a little more than three hundred more in a bee line, but nearer five hundred by the route and in the manner

he was compelled to go. So far his success had been
encouraging. Should it continue he felt confident of
accomplishing his task. Those six days had accomplished a wonderful change in him. He was ragged
and dirty, and no longer cared for appearances. He
was now an expert in stealing rides. There was a
bold, lawless, vagabond feeling gaining an ascendancy
over him. He was fast losing the self respect that
cares for the opinions of others. His stomach had
accustomed itself to the new *regime.* He ate vora-
ciously when he could obtain food in plenty, and
found himself fasting an entire twenty-four hours
without any very disagreeable sensations. He was no
longer afraid to ask for food, nor ashamed of being
ordered roughly from a train or its vicinity. He cared
nothing about the stares with which he was greeted;
an Ishmaelitish feeling was growing upon him — and
he did not care to repress it. In fact Ben had become
a *tramp.*

His new companion, the Evangelist, was a sociable,
easy-going, good-natured fellow. He had traits that
were peculiar. Differing from the majority of tramps,
he never uttered an oath. "I promised my dear,
good mother, when a child, that I would not swear,
and I never have," he said.

His love and respect for his mother's memory was
something sublime, amid his rags and degradation.
He never spoke disrespectfully of her sex, nor would
he allow others to. He mentioned her often in the
most devoted manner, and it was easy to be seen that
she was the idol of his life. Though a cynic and a
skeptic he once said to Ben :

" Were I positive that there was no hereafter, I
would school myself to think otherwise. For of what
use would life be to me did I not have the hope of
again being by the side of her who has gone before
me ? " And on another occasion he said :

" I like free-thinkers well enough, and freedom of
thought. I would not that any one should be bound
down to the slavery of creed or dogma. Nor do I
believe that any one poor, weak piece of human clay
has a right to dictate the road to immortality, or sit
in judgment on a fellow being. But he who wrecks
a comforting belief or destroys a solacing faith, ruins
that which he cannot replace. He takes away a happiness and offers nothing in return. It is a despicable
act. A man had better let the creed or faith of his
neighbor alone."

Horton had no aims, no ambitions, no aspirations.
His was a harmless, purposeless life. An inoffensive
vagabond who first excited your contempt, and then
won your pity. His mother had been left a widow,
in poverty, when he was a babe, and with her needle,
supported herself and child. All her mother's hopes
were centered in him ; all his childish love in her.
She struggled hard to give him a fair education, and
the happiest moment of her life was when her boy entered a theological seminary. Up to that time Horton had been a more than usually bright and promising boy. Whatever he did was done " for mother's
sake," and all his air-castles were occupied by her.
While he was at the seminary she died, and he never
recovered from the blow. A dull, dead apathy to all
about him was succeeded by a mild cynicism and a sad

rebellion against the justice of Providence; which latter caused his speedy expulsion from the theological school, about which he cared nothing, however.

"Why could not my mother have been left to me?" he would say. "Had not sorrows, toils and trials enough been heaped upon her dear head, but that just as I was becoming a value and a consolation to her she must be taken from me and I from her?"

When told that "the Lord chasteneth those he loveth," he would bitterly exclaim:

"Then I want nothing to do with such a God! It is man's God. Created by himself, and like himself, a thing of fury and vengeance! No, no, no. Him who lights the stars in the sky, and in whose hand this world is a mite so small that his Almighty eye alone can see it, is not the base, slaughter-thirsty creation poor, weak mortals attempt to depict in words that flavor of the dust of earth and thoughts that cannot go beyond the grave!"

It was probably a lack of discretion on his part, and a pernicious habit of speaking out his thoughts, that brought Horton into disrepute with respectable people when he chanced to stop among them. For men and women do not like to have people — especially poor and dependent people — set up in the thinking business for themselves, while so much labor and money has been expended to have their thinking done for them; it looks presumptuous and ungrateful.

The Evangelist had an old silver watch that had belonged to his father. It had been the family time piece of the little home formed by his adored mother and himself, and through all the vicissitudes of his rambling life he had managed to retain it. It was the connecting link between himself and a past respectability.

Ben had taken a great liking to the fellow, and often spoke to him seriously about reforming his vagabond career, and becoming a decent member of society. But Horton's sophistry was too much for him.

" Drones are not the worst inhabitants of this great hive, called the world," he would say laughingly. " Drones are consumers, and the more consumers and fewer producers, the better times are. This country was never so busy at work as when it had a million of non-productive men in the field, to take care of. As a vagabond, I support others by compelling others to support me."

Ben's words evidently at times had some effect on him, however, and set him to doing much quiet thinking.

CHAPTER XVI.

THE EVANGELIST INVESTS IN A HORSE.

A RATHER unprofitable journey by daylight was attempted, with but little success. The trains were so closely watched that they found it next to impossible to ride on them. Some tramps, whom they met on foot, informed them that this was on account of a fracas that had occurred on the western end of the line. The train men were expelling some free-riders, and handling one of them very roughly the tramp drew a knife and plunged it into the side of a brakeman. The wounded man was not expected to recover, and very strict orders had been issued by the management of the road to prevent all tramps from boarding trains or riding upon them.

This being the case the Evangelist suggested that they strike across the country, and get on another railroad, running nearly parallel, fifty miles to the south of them.

They walked quite a distance that evening, and camped in a straw pile. On the following day they resumed their line of march through a lovely rolling country of openings, woodlands and meadows, inter-spersed by many streams.

It was the middle of September — the golden time of all the year. The atmosphere was filled with a soft, hazy lustre; the reflex heat of the summer months after it had journeyed so far as the ice fields of the far north, and been turned back in a soft and gracious air. Gentle winds told forest tales among the tall trees, and nodded the heads of the grey mullens in requiem over the great, broad, plush-like leaves that lay dying at the foot of the stalks. Sentinel sheaves of wheat stood grouped about the yellow fields, and from out the stubble came the piping of the quail mingling with the rustling of the long, drooping, corn leaves; a mellow, autumnal refrain. Near at hand the chattering brook ran a messenger of harvest time to the far off river, and the river carried the news to the gulf, and the gulf swept it to the four corners of the earth.

> " As printed staves of thankful Nature's hymn,
>   The fence of rails a soothing grace devotes,   /
>   With clinging vines for bass and treble cleffs,
>   And wrens and robins here and there for notes ;
>   Spread out in bars, at equal distance met,
>   As though the whole bright autumn scene were set
>   To the unuttered melody of Rest ! "

> " The mill-wheel motionless o'ershades the pool,
>   In whose frail crystal cups its circle dips ;
>   The stream, slow-curling, wanders in the sun,
>   And drains his kisses with its silver lips ;
>   The birch canoe upon its shadow lies,
>   The pike's last bubble on the water dies,
>   The water lily sleeps upon her glass."

The lovely quiet of the country gave our travellers a feeling of peace and rest, that the sharp voice of the iron horse and the rattle of his steel-shod hoofs had forbidden them.

THE EVANGELIST INVESTS IN A HORSE. 137

"This it is that makes tramping glorious!" exclaimed the Evangelist, imbued with the beauty and placidity of Nature's feast.

"'Far from the maddening crowd's ignoble strife' I could tramp forever and forever, with Nature for a companion, and feed my hungry eyes on her loveliness!"

Toward the close of the afternoon, as Ben and his friend were seated, resting on the top rail of an old, moss-covered, stake-and-rider fence, a young man came up to them mounted on a horse. The animal was without a saddle and looked as though he had been severely ridden. His rider appeared to be an ordinary young country fellow, without any particular points of interest about him. He drew rein opposite our friends and entered into conversation with them, stating that he was a resident of Bonfield in the adjoining county, thirty miles distant, and having had a falling out with the old folks at home, had left the parental roof with this horse — his only property — determined to seek his fortunes abroad ; ef it tuk him through six 'jining counties! But he found the horse to be a plaguy botheration. He'd no saddle, an' he was too poor to buy one, and too poor to afford the luxury of a ridin'. He could better afford to walk. He said he was a simple feller and didn't know much 'bout the world, no how, which they might a seed. He was detarmined to sell or dicker his hoss, and mebbe they'd like to buy the anamyle. How much w'uld they give fur him ? But our friends had no money to purchase him with even had they been so inclined. In that case moughtn't they hev sumthin'

they'd trade ?   For the rider was so durned tired
of the bruit, durned if he didn't nigh feel like
givin' him away, or a tradin' him fur sum durned
jack knife !   Our friends had nothing to trade him,
however.

No pistols, nor watches, nor jewelry, nor nothing?

Ben shook his head, but the Evangelist studied a
moment.

"Ben," he whispered, "I hate to part with my
watch. It is the last earthly tie I have binding me
to memories of the past. But — if — if I had that
horse I could sell him — sell him may be for fifty or
sixty dollars ! And that would be money enough to
take us both decently to St. Louis, and pay our expenses there until we could secure employment —
good employment. I'd give up rambling, and — it
might be the making of us both ! "

Cleveland tried to persuade him not to part with
the watch, but the sanguine temperament of the Evangelist — peculiar to him — was already picturing a
life of respectability in St. Louis. A great reforma-
tion with Ben for a constant moral support to lean
upon. Indeed it was Ben's own reasoning heretofore
that caused the other to think at all of changing his
condition.

" Yes I will, yes I will, Ben. It's a great chance
— who knows what may come of it ! "

And Ben who had formed a strong liking for his
companion thought perhaps it might be for the best
after all. That it might, possibly, be a turning point
in Horton's life, that would redeem him.

The watch was scarce worth twenty dollars. It

had heavy, old-fashioned silver cases, but the works — though in good order — were antique. Horton offered it to the rider for his horse, and the latter, after dickering for something " to boot," and finding he could get nothing more, accepted it. Then he transferred the horse to the Evangelist, calling upon Ben to be a witness to the trade, and bidding our friends good day, stated that he wished to pass the night with a cousin six miles distant, and struck out over the fields.

The two travellers took a look at their new acquisition. He wās a trifle old, and had a bone spavin, but otherwise was a good, solid chunk of a farm horse. The question now arose what to do with him.

"I'll tell you," said Horton, "it is about twelve miles to Lickskillet, where we strike the railroad. That is too far for you to walk to-night, but I can ride, and get into the town an hour or so before sundown, by pushing my horse. I'll sell him there for all I can get, and wait for you. You walk so far as you feel able to-night and get up early to-morrow morning and come on," and then after a pause: " Don't delay Ben, for it aint just safe for me to have money about me yet — my good resolutions are too new," and he laughed, but his voice was serious and entreating.

This arrangement being perfected the Evangelist mounted his purchase and rode off at a sharp canter, Ben following more slowly on foot.

Now that Horton was gone our hero discovered what a companion he had been. Always ready with

some quaint suggestion or far-fetched argument —
original in his metaphors and epigrammatic in his
criticisms — he had caused the time to pass away
agreeably, and Ben missed him.

With pleasant reveries he beguiled the way until
sundown came upon him unnoticed. He could have
made Lickskillet that night by an increase of exertion, but his feet were tired and as there was no necessity for getting into the town until morning, he
began looking about him for a camping place. While
prospecting for a straw pile, or hay stack, suitably situated for his night's rest, he passed a comfortable
farm house, consisting of a frame building with a log
kitchen in its rear. In the barn yard, near the house,
a man was attempting to raise a corn crib by means
of two timbers used as levers. The method did not
appear to work well, and Ben watched him through
several failures. He would first bear down one of his
levers, and piling stones upon it attempt to hold it in
this manner, while he lifted on the other. But the
levers slipped, and he was unsuccessful. He had
worked fruitlessly long enough to make help appreciated, and when Ben offered his assistance, it was
gladly accepted. It took nearly an hour's labor to
get the corn crib into the desired position and prop-
erly propped up.

When the work was done, the farmer thanked him
and asked if he was travelling.

"Yes, sir; I'm on my way to St. Louis."

"Wall, I declar! Reckon you'll git thar twixt
now and Chris'mas?"

Ben reckoned he would.

"I declar! No money?"

"No money."

"Turrible bad condition, I declar! Come in and take a bite; ye've arned yer supper. I ain't got no great show of 'commodations, but these nights air not cold, an' thar's a plenty of fresh straw out in the cow shed. Reckon ye kin make out? Hey, not?"

Ben assured him that the accommodations offered were highly acceptable.

"And whar mought ye come frum?" asked the farmer.

"New York," replied Ben.

"I declar! State or city?"

"City."

"I declar!" And he looked at Ben and Ben looked at him. "That's a right smart piece frum hyar, I reckon?"

Ben told him it was nearly eight hundred miles, at which he "declar'd!" again.

On entering the farm house he was introduced to the farmer's wife, and four small tow-headed children, with the remark:

"Fly round, 'Riah; hyar's a man all the way frum New Yurk City agoin' to St. Lowis; an' I'm turrible peckish, which I reckon he is too," at which 'Riah also said "I declar!" and the four tow-headed children stood with open mouths and looked it, though they did not say so.

At the table the farmer turned to Ben, somewhat to the latter's consternation, and asked:

"Strangier, will you say a blessin'?"

Ben might have recited some Homeric ode, but a simple blessing left him high and dry on the shoals of ignorance, and he had to decline.

The good man came near saying " I declar!" but corrected himself, and proceeded to ask divine protection for himself and family and the stranger within his gates, interpolating a few reflections upon his oldest son and heir's reprehensible act of sticking his fingers in the "meat gravy," and introducing in the invocation a promise to give the two youngest tow heads " a good larrupin' fur their obstreporosity of behaviour." Grace having been duly wound up by the head of the family smartly rapping the tow head nearest to him with his knuckles, for an infraction of proprieties, Ben was solicited not to stand on ceremony, but to " pitch in."

After supper a pipe and a chat by a log fire — more for light and cheerfulness than heat — followed. But our hero soon grew sleepy, tired out with the day's long walk, and retired to the cow shed determined to be up and away at early cock crow in the morning.

Sometime during the night he was partially awakened from his slumbers by voices on the kitchen porch. Half asleep and half awake he heard the following disjointed expressions :

" He's caught — Lickskillet jail — they're all a coming — 'greed to it after meetin' — make an example of him — we'll show 'em — come on — be quick!" After which he was dimly conscious that some one entered the barn and saddled a horse. There was a clatter of hoofs out on the road, and then all was again quiet, and Ben slept peacefully.

It was the dark hour before dawn when the restless chanticleer from his perch in a neighboring apple tree called our hero up. He limbered himself with a good round of shakes and stamping life into his sleepy feet, started out in the dark for Lickskillet, five miles distant.

CHAPTER XVII.

LICKSKILLET HAS A SENSATION.

THOUGH this is a true and faithful chronicle of the adventures of our friend Benjamin Cleveland, so closely have his affairs now become linked with the destiny of another that we must temporarily leave him, and turn to the hamlet of Lickskillet.

When the Evangelist arrived with his horse late the previous afternoon, he found the village to consist of a single straggling street, lined by country stores, in front of which were hitched a few farm teams and country wagons. The Evangelist was stared at after the usual bucolic fashion. His immediate business being the disposal of his equine property, he rode up to a long, low, weather-stained building, bearing the legend, "Livery, board and sale stable," in skeleton characters on a board that decorated a pole. Half a dozen loungers greeted his advent with a stolid stare.

Horton rode into the building and dismounting, propounded the question:

"Does anybody know of anybody that wants to buy a horse?"

Another stare, more dense in its stupidity and stolidity, greeted the query.

"If they do, here's a solid good work horse I'll sell cheap," continued he.

At this information a man, who had been engaging his time and attention in company with an intelligent jack knife, upon a shingle, arose, and allowing his hand and knife to pare away at the wood after their own inclination, walked slowly around the horse and observed him with a critical eye.

" Whar'd ye get him ? " he asked.

" Bought him of a man up the road," replied Horton. " I got him at a bargain, and I'll sell him at one."

" How much ? " asked the man.

" I'll sell him for fifty dollars, cash," said the Evangelist.

The man stared at Horton a full minute without speaking, slowly running his eye from the Evangelist's head to his feet and up again several times. Then, still whittling, he walked to the barn door, where he turned and gave a sly wink to one of the stolid men present ; which pantomimic piece of activity seemed to create some little sensation among the human stolidity present.

One after another they arose, and slowly walking around the horse, eyed him from head to tail, then giving Horton a final examination, passed quietly out of the door, until the latter found himself left alone with his horse.

This situation lasted but a few moments, for the man who first went out shortly returned, still whittling, and commenced interrogating him.

" Whar did ye kum frum ? Whar air ye goin' ?

How long ye hed the animyle? Wot ye want to sell
it fur? How'd he kum to be rid so hard?" and numerous other questions were asked and duly answered.
Having finished his category, the stable-keeper — for
it was the owner and proprietor of the "livery" — remarked:

"Looks mighty 'spicious!"

"What looks suspicious?" asked Horton.

"Oh, nothing," replied the man with a tone and
look indicating that his yahoo mind was one immense
volume of doubt.

The Evangelist was puzzled. He could see nothing strange about the matter, and so expressed himself. If a man wanted a good horse cheap, there was
the animal — and if he did not, he could let it alone.
A liberty of action that would no doubt have power-
fully impressed the "'spicious" man were it not that
the attention of both was suddenly diverted into other
channels. There were heard the murmur of many
voices, and the shuffling of many feet on the street,
and half a hundred men, picked up from farmers'
wagons, trading stores and adjacent fields, rushed into
the stable and surrounded Horton and the horse.
While he was staring in astonishment at this influx
of purchasers, a lank, sandy-complexioned man stepped
from the crowd and taking one look at the horse, exclaimed:

"That's him! Whoa, Bob!"

The animal immediately recognizing the voice and
name, turned his head and greeted the sandy man
with a neigh.

At this Horton stepped back in astonishment, but

the next instant was felled to the stable floor by a blow on the head, and three men pounced upon him, crying out:

" No you don't, you scoundrel! You're too late! We've got ye and'll keep ye! You bet!"

" Gentlemen," cried the Evangelist so soon as he could recover breath, " What in the name of Heaven does all this mean?"

" Mean!" exclaimed half a dozen voices, while a score of angry eyes glared vengefully upon him; " Mean? Why it means ye're gone up, ye whelp of a hoss thief!"

" I am no thief!" he indignantly replied. " That horse is my property, and I came by him honestly."

" Ye lie!" shouted he of the sandy complexion, who was now holding ' Bob.' " Ye lie! Ye stole that hoss outer my cow lot night afore last. I kem from Spoonerville down the town-line rud or I'd hev cot ye on the way, an' ef I hed the county ud hev been saved the expense of yer trial!" And giving utterance to this dark shadowing of a vengeful purpose the sandy man glared upon Horton.

" Gentlemen it is *false!* I — " commenced the Evangelist, but the sandy man, unable to reach him with his hands and hold his horse at the same time, gave the poor captive a vicious kick in the stomach, exclaiming:

" Ye mean to tell me *I lie*, ye dirty, hoss thief!"

One would have thought that in that crowd some voice had been found to call " shame " at the cow-ardly act of striking a man held from self defence by the hands of others. But the agricultural sense of honôr is somewhat like the agricultural habits of life — somewhat narrowed by limited associations. Had the good feelings of the crowd been appealed to they would all have rushed after a leader like a flock of sheep, probably. It being the opposite, Horton was kicked and cuffed to their heart's content, as though each had a private grievance to attend to. They then stood him on his feet and demanded that he give an account of himself.

Thoroughly frightened and suffering much pain from the harsh treatment he had received, and fearing a repetition of it that seemed to indicate itself in the lowering looks surrounding him, the poor unfortunate Evangelist humbled his tone, and gave a truthful statement of himself and the manner in which he had obtained possession of the horse. Briefly he stated who he was and did not try to palliate the crime of being a tramp. Then he related how, while in company with Ben, he had traded a watch for the horse with a farmer's boy who lived in Bonfield, and had brought the animal in town to sell it; leaving his comrade back on the road, to come after him on the morrow.

" A likely story ! "

" Did he think to stuff that down their throats ? "

" A man without money having watches to give for horses ! Too thin ! "

" Where was his partner ? "

" Selling another horse somewhere, probably ! "

" He said he was a tramp, and what was a tramp but a hoss thief ! "

And they laughed at his statements in derision.

The tide was setting strong against the Evangelist. It became a perfect torrent when the sandy complexioned man called upon another sandy complexioned man, with sandy hair and sandy beard and sandy clothes, and small sandy blue eyes, and hard sandy hands (honest, no doubt, but very ragged at the finger ends and very dirt-grimed) and a sandy voice, and sandy appearance generally from his heel to his occiput, to come take a good "squar" look at Horton, and see if he was not the man he had seen loafing around in the vicinity of Spoonerville? And this sandiest of all sandy men, feeling himself elevated to a consequential position, felt it incumbent upon his new notoriety to aver that Horton was the man; compromising with some slight qualms of conscience with the codicil that " leastways he *luks* mighty sight like him." That settled it. And all his wild protestations could not change the decision of the crowd that immediately transformed the luckless Evangelist from a tramp into a horse thief.

By this time a man who was duly authorized to act as town marshal appeared on the scene, and with a deal of importance seized Horton's person in the majestic name of the Law! and conveyed his seizure, followed by the crowd, to the village lock-up. A small plank box, twelve feet by twelve feet in all of its dimensions, without a window, and principally used for the occasional cooling off of· some obstreperous bucolics who on coming to town became surcharged with the staff of life in a liquid form. Into this hole, standing solitary and alone in the centre of the village common, he was thrown, and the door closed with a bang. The rusty key grated in the rusty lock, the rusty crowd outside gave some rusty whoops and yells, and then went off pawing the air as men who had done great deeds. It was as though, in some far off Hindoo village, the tiger that had been fattening his ribs upon the natives had at last been caught and caged. Everybody, save that poor battered and bruised form on the floor of the village lockup, was triumphant!

And now of what use is a triumph unless we celebrate it? And what is the great American method of celebrating triumphs? From the nabob who in gilded apartments gracefully nods his head to his brother nabob, as he remarks: " I congratulate you " before sending the soul of sunny France gurgling down his pink throat, down to the ragged effigy who leans against the sour-smelling fetid bar and cracks his glass against the glass of his brother effigy, with: " Here's luck, d — n your soul! " as he pitches the scorching tanglefoot down his red hot gullet, we Americans have our own method of celebrating triumphs. We get drunk.

So these Lickskilletonians celebrated in the hour of their triumph.

Stiff, sore, bruised, battered and bleeding, the Evangelist struggled to his feet and staggering to a narrow, iron-barred slit in the side of the village lockup, looked out. The sun was creeping to bed among the purple hills of the horizon. Already it had nearly disappeared; all save a narrow disk, that with a red, autumnal glow was bidding the world good-night. Long and earnestly he gazed upon the glowing west,

painted with red and purple and russet, and trimmed
with silver and gold. With its woods and meadows
and vales, painted by God's own hand. With its fading lights, its deepening shadows, its soft grey of coming twilight. Long he gazed, until the shadows had
swallowed up the light, and the grey of twilight was
lost in the dusk of night. Then he flung himself on
the floor, and sleep came with a soft and soothing
balm to anoint his wounds ; his eyes filled with that
last glow — *his last* — of his Creator's sunlight.

CHAPTER XVIII.

JUDGE LYNCH HOLDS COURT.

A SHORT distance out of Lickskillet stood a country church. A quiet-looking, unpretentious frame building, with a stunted little steeple surmounted by a weather-vane in the shape of an arrow hanging at right angles on an iron rod with a gilded point. The weekly prayer meeting was being held that evening, and the yeomen of the vicinity met to send their appeals for clemency, in a body, to the Great Judge on high ; each taking his turn in the supplications. A sort of prayerful round-robin. An opportunity to improve the recording angel's record in the celestial ledger, and enhance their reputations for goodness among the neighbors by a full, (but inexpensive,) confession of their sins and wickedness. Confessions on general principles, however — not specific ones. Brother Longhorn prayed for forgiveness for his sins in general, but did not mention defrauding Green Southdown in a horse trade, nor did he speak any thing about restitution. Brother Ploughgit demanded that the wicked be no longer allowed to flourish like the green bay tree — and did not tremble

with personal apprehension while doing it. Brother
Hedges took much satisfaction in announcing that he
was a poor, weak sinner — which confession was apparently concurred in by a number of the brethren.
Brother Ryefield spoke glowingly of charity and
prayed that they all might be greatly blessed with
that virtue — but said nothing about withdrawing a
suit against a man who was trying to support a wife,
five children, and the consumption on nothing.
Brother Powter wanted strength to do His bidding,
which caused Brother Applegate to reflect that if His
bidding conflicted with Brother Powter's *own* bidding
it would take all the strength of sixteen hundred
million yoke of fat cattle to answer Brother Powter's
prayer. Brother Potts was thankful for what he had
and wanted more. Brother Rockafellow prayed that
their hearts might all be filled with an abiding peace
and love. And they all say " Amen ! "

After meeting the general topic was the capture of
the horse thief. Down in the village the unregener-
ated were still holding a feeble celebration, but beyond
an excuse for celebrating they did not look upon the
capture as an incentive to sterner action. Not so
with the brethren. They did not endorse the celebration. That is, not publicly. Moreover they
looked upon the celebrants as a vain and worldly people.

But at a cross road Brother Powter met Brother
Longhorn, and was overtaken by Brother Rockafellow and Brother Ploughgit and Brother Hedges, and
several other brothers, and a discussion ensued as to
the safety of live stock in that vicinity — more especially " hosses."

" I tell ye wot," said Brother Powter, "this thing's got to be stopped. We aint none of us safe ! "

" An' I don't see but now's the 'pinted time to stop it," said Brother Rockafellow.

And Brother Longhorn said :

" Ef we make a example of this one, it'll clear the country of the scoundrils an' give us peace an' security ! "

" But mebbe the lor hed better take its course," suggested a timid brother.

" Thet's it Brother Calfer; thet's it. Wot is the course of the lor? Why it's to involve the county hed over ears in debts fur us farmers to pay, an' let the hoss thief go free ! Thet's wot the lor is ! " and this explanation of what the law consisted of met with many approving expressions of " Thet's so ! " " You've hit it ! " " Lor's a swindle ! " " Ropes good cheap lor ! " and other endorsements.

And the little crowd at the cross roads in caucus assembled appointed each one present a committee of one to ride around the neighborhood that night and invite the neighbors to meet before "sun up" on the public square in Lickskillet, and " devise measures for the protection of the public peace and property, more especially hosses."

On the cold floor of his prison the Evangelist lay folded in the arms of the merciful angel of rest. The blood had dried upon his face, and its deep crimson contrasted weirdly with the ghastly palor of his countenance even in the faint star light that crept through the one narrow aperture in the building. His long, thin fingers were clasped as though in prayer, and

ever and anon his lips would move and a smile break
upon them — hideously out of conformity with his
blood-stained face.   But blood and wounds and bruises
and rags and miseries and wretchedness, were all for-
gotten by the sleeper.   He was with his mother.   He
was with her, in that realm entered only through the
portals of sleep.   Again he was a boy.   Again with
dog-eared books flung over his shoulder, he saun-
tered down the green New England lane ; — rich in
the glories of wild-roses and gaudy thistle-blossoms ;
odor-ladened by groups of cedar bushes and the mellow fragrance of old orchards, tuned to harmony with
the chatter of blue jays and the operatic notes of bob-
olinks.   Here a pebble to kick, there a mullen head
to switch from its stalk ; now a puff-ball to crush
with his heel, a rabbit to chase in the brush, and an
old post to lean against with hands in pockets and
books flung at his feet, while he looked and whistled
and whistled and looked, just in sheer glee and relief
that the day's work in the weather-stained school-
house was over.   Then a shout and a run down the
low hill that ended by the cottage gate, where a thin
care-worn woman, with fond eyes, wrapped him in her
arms and pressed her lips lovingly to his — joyed with
him in his joys and sorrowed with him in his sorrows.
No wonder that the lips of him who lay on the hard
floor of the Lickskillet lockup murmured the name
of " *Mother*."   The purest, truest, holiest being that
the heart of man ever enshrined for its idol !

But what is this ?   There is the noise of many
voices without — a rush of many feet.   The door of
his prison resounds to a heavy blow.   The sharp point

of an iron bar is thrust between the jamb and the lock. It shivers and groans with the pressure. Groans as if in protest against the violence about to be committed. Then, with a grinding screech, it flies open and the Evangelist springs to his feet. Springs to his feet to be confronted by a judge from whose decision there is no appeal. A judge whose court has flooded this fair land with scenes of blood and murder. A judge whose jury is the brute passions of mankind. The abettor of spite, vengeance, ignorance and bigotry. A judge who knows no law save the law of *might*. A judge who held his court on the steps of the guillotine, in the mountain haunts of the Covenanters, and in the streets of old Venice. A judge, who when banished in loathing from the old world, brought his dread court to the new, and treads the civilization, the Christianity and the progress of the nineteenth century beneath his heel in this fair land. A judge who daily calls upon us/ by his acts, cited in the public press, to rise and hurl him from his bench, and declare ourselves at last on a level with the enlightened nations of the earth. JUDGE LYNCH!

As Horton arose to his feet he encountered this hideous parody upon civilization in the shape of two hundred maddened men. Maddened with a thirst for human life.

"Come out hyar!" yelled the mob.

" Bring him out! Bring him out! Hang the hoss thief! Shoot him! We'll rid the country of him! Rope him! Rope him!" they cried.

There were many men in the crowd, who in calm reflective moments would have shrunk from a deed of violence. But they were wild. Wild with excitement. Wild with the darkness of night. Wild with a self-heated anger. Wild with the horribly fantastic knowledge that a human life was in their hands to do just as they pleased with. To crush, to destroy, to *hang* — and none to say them nay.

" For God's sake, gentlemen, what will you do with me ? " cried the Evangelist.

" We'll show you ! We'll teach you to steal hosses ! " they yelled for an answer.

" I did not steal ! As God is my witness I am no thief. Time will prove it. Will you not give me a chance for my life ? " he pleaded wildly.

" Dry up ! No use lying now ! We know what kind of watches you fellers trade for hosses ! " and a loud laugh greeted this last witticism.

Four men seized the protesting man and running as many ropes about his neck, they started off, dragging him along the road in the clear starlight, the crowd following hooting and yelling. The ropes tightened around his throat, and it was with the utmost difficulty he kept himself from being strangled. Speak he could not, though every atom of his body was in a dreadful quiver with that appalling sensation which those who have approached close to a horrible and unexpected death alone can realize or understand.

Yelling, hooting and jeering, the crowd dragged him out of the village to the patch of woods near the country church. Every thing was done hurriedly. A man climbed an oak tree and flung a rope over a sturdy limb into the hands of those below. At this moment the Evangelist found tongue.

" Men !" he exclaimed. "Men or brutes ! This
is murder ! *Murder !* I am as guiltless of stealing
that horse as the child unborn. I have told you truthfully how I came by it. Will you kill me thus without allowing me to prove my innocence? *Are* you
men, are you human, are you Christians? Will you
deliberately take my blood upon your hands ? "

But a voice replied, and it sounded like that of
Brother Rockafellow, though the man had a handkerchief tied over his face, partly concealing it :

" Strangier, make yer peace with the Lord. Thar's
even marcy fur such as you, perhaps. Hev ye the
rope ready ? "

At this moment a new comer appeared on the
scene. It was the lank, thin, care-worn pastor of the
little church ; the shepherd of this thirsty flock. The
noise had aroused him in his faded cottage, and in
great perturbation and much trembling of his bony
limbs, and rubbing of his withered hands he approached to see what it was all about.

" It's a hoss thief, an' in a minit we're going to hev
one less in the kentry," explained the mob.

Instantly the thin, lank, trembling pastor was transformed into an iron-nerved, fearless warrior of the
Master's army.

" Men," he cried, and his thin voice fairly reached
a shriek with the unaccustomed energy ; "men, you
shall *not* kill the man ! Vengeance is *mine*, saith the
Lord ! A murderer shall not enter the kingdom of
heaven, and you are committing murder ! In the
name of Jesus I implore you to stop. Hold on. Let
me alone. Release me. I *will* get to him. You are

savages. How dare you, sir! Don't kill him. Stop, stop!" and hustled back by the crowd, this soul, worthier of a nobler tenement, went down on his knees and begged and prayed that they would hold their vengeful hands.

"He'll not preach here no more." "We've done with him." "Conference will hev to give us another preacher." "Make the durned old fool shet up," and similar hostile expressions were unheard or unheeded. He reproached, begged, threatened, implored. All was wasted upon the crowd. The tiger was loose. He had wetted his lips in imagination, was he to be cheated of his prey? The good man's protestations and supplications were alike disregarded.

"At least let me pray with him. Let me give him the consolation of our blessed Lord and Saviour in these, his last moments upon earth," he implored.

This request was at first refused, but ultimately reluctantly granted, with the observation that they could not see what the old idiot wanted to make so much fuss over a durned hoss thief for. The good man shook Horton by the hand, and spoke consolingly to him, giving him such sympathy as he could, and begging him to turn his thoughts on Him who died for all.

A great change had come over the Evangelist. He no longer supplicated for life, nor indeed did he pay much attention to those around him. Perhaps he saw how useless it was to search for their feelings. Perchance his thoughts were far away and death had lost its terrors. To a question of his only friend he replied:

"No, I have no relatives. There are none that I would care to acquaint with my fate. But I am an innocent man. Here, standing on the brink of Eternity, without a hope for this world, about to be ushered, all unheralded, all unsummoned, into the presence of Him who gave me life, I would not deceive you. I am innocent. And I solemnly adjure you at whose hands I perish that in the future, when you have found out the mistake of your crime, that it shall ever be a warning to you to hold more sacred that life which God has given, and which, though you may take, you cannot replace. And may He forgive you as I forgive you."

A man now flung the noose of the rope over his head. Others roughly ordered the minister out of the way, and the good man affectionately embracing Horton and bidding him good-bye, retreated to the church steps, and seating himself, with face upturned and eyes flowing tears, sang in a thin treble voice:

"Jesus, Saviour of my soul,
Let me to thy bosom fly."

At the moment the rope was tightening on the victim's neck, there occurred a commotion on the outer edge of the crowd, and breathless and hatless Ben forced his way through and up to the unfortunate companion of his wanderings.

"Hold!" he cried, "hold! This man is innocent. I was with him when he traded his watch for that horse. You are murdering an innocent man!"

"Who're you?" roughly enquired a number.

"He's the man who was with me when I got the horse; the man I told you of. He will prove that I did not steal it," calmly replied Horton.

" That's a likely story ! " exclaimed a voice.

" Thief a helpin' thief ! " shouted another.

" He's another hoss thief ! "

" We've got 'em both ! Hang 'em both ! Make a clean sweep and clean the kentry of them ! " yelled the crowd.

" I am no thief ! " cried Ben. " My name is Benjamin Cleveland. Boston is my home. I am walking to New Orleans on a wager. You can prove it by telegraph and hang me if it is not so."

A derisive laugh greeted this information.

" Walkin' to New Orleans, air ye ? Well ye'll hev to walk another route, and a warmer one ! "

" Rope him ! Rope him ! Let's clean the State of the villains, and leave 'em hanging up as a warning ! "

As this was shouted Ben felt a rope thrown over his neck, and the next instant both he and the Evangelist were jerked into the air amid a chorus of yells. There was a confused murmur of voices beneath him. He struggled and kicked. Tried to loose the rope that was strangling him with his hands. The froth oozed from his mouth. The confined blood seemed bursting his head. Ten thousand bells were clanging in his ears. He tried to cry out. A low gurgle escaped him. Then all grew black and blank.

When Ben regained consciousness he was lying at the foot of the oak tree with a loosened rope around his neck. His head seemed gigantic in its size and his lips were parched. The grey light of morning was struggling over the eastern hills. Not a soul was in sight. No, — *not a soul.*

But turning his eyes upward they encountered a sight that caused him to close them again with a groan of horror. For there, swinging gently to and fro, in the morning breeze, hung the stiff, lifeless body of Horton the Evangelist. His eyes bulging from their sockets, his swollen tongue protruding from his mouth, and his gaunt face tinted with the leaden palor of stagnant blood.

Dead! Hung by the neck. Dead!

As the eye of God came grandly up over the eastern horizon, it glanced upon awakening nature, and fell upon that hideous, untenanted clod of abused clay, that gently swung from the sturdy oak. And as it glanced on the ruin and devastation the little church fell in its way. And it took the shadow of the steeple along over the road and over the open space, to the woods, clean to the foot of the oak tree, up which it pointed like some avenging finger. Up and still up crept the shadow until it reached the body of the dead man with the weather vane. And, Lo! When Ben again dared to lift his eyes, there, on the stark, still, pulseless breast of the Evangelist, was THE SHADOW OF THE CROSS!"

CHAPTER XIX.

THE GREAT HARVEST RANGE.

TURN we now to record more grateful scenes. Let us leave the black cross on the breast of the dead man. The dead man swinging in the morning breeze. Our backs are turned upon an unknown, moundless grave, down in a sandy, barren jack-oak field. A shallow grave over which no head stone tells the passer by that all flesh is grass. A grave on which the startled rabbit pauses, with ears erect, to heed the breaking of a twig. A grave on which the quail pipes forth his cheering notes in the glimmer of the dawn, and the prairie grouse crows good night to the setting sun. A grave in which lies mouldering a monument to the reign of the lawless judge. A grave in which is secreted the prey of the human tiger. The occupant of the grave has found rest at last. His tramp is o'er. He sleeps the sleep that knows no waking, he dreams the dream that knows no breaking.

That there is only one occupant of the shallow grave down in the black-jack barren is due to the exertions of the man with whom Ben ate supper the previous evening. He it was who extended aid to our hero in his dire distress and saved his life. Through his intercessions Cleveland was lowered from the limb and spared. Like one walking in his sleep, his mind and energies paralyzed by the dreadful scene through which he had passed, Ben made a futile attempt to justify his dead friend's memory. He only met with repulses — nay, threats. No one would believe him, none give credence to his tale. He found none who had witnessed the hanging, none who would talk about it, but plenty who with frowning eyes and threatening looks turned their backs upon him when he attempted to speak of it. Had Ben appeared before that bulwark of the law — that greatest of all great American impositions — the Grand Jury, and told his tale of the *crime*, the Grand Jury could not have laid its indicting hand on a single man who had had any thing to do with the hanging. He did not know this, nor did he appreciate the people he was among. He called for justice, and came near getting a flogging. One not unfavorable result was accomplished by his pertinacious search after justification, however. Though he did not find the blind goddess, he found a railway ticket that conveyed him out of the State, and two hundred miles westward. His presence became disagreeable to the citizens of Lickskillet. The tiger had glutted himself and was drowsy. He did not like to be disturbed.

A delegation of two benevolent citizens waited upon him and informed him that from the plentitude of their hearts, and the charitable nature of their dispositions they were not only willing to condone his recent acts and view his crimes with a lenient eye, but they would aid him on his journey, and provide him with a railroad ticket to a distant point, with the stipulation that his foot should never press their sod again, and a gentle intimation that his own particular rope would be carefully preserved for his own particular use. The offer came in the shape of a command. With a stubbornness, peculiarly his own, Ben would have rejected it. He would have staid and fought to the death there and then for his dead friend's memory. But the poor, thin, lank parson came to him. The good man trembled lest the tiger should be roused from his slumber. He knew the beast for had he not dwelt beneath the velvet of its paw for many a day? He demonstrated to our hero the futility of one man, and he a penniless stranger, attempting the indictment of an entire community bound together by ties of blood, relationship, interest and — *crime*. A community that was a law unto it-self. Ben gathered a clearer view of the case from the good man's explanations.

So Ben was placed on board of a train, and whirled away into Egypt.

Or, to speak more lucidly, into the very centre of Southern Illinois. And despite the sad incidents that had thronged the past forty-eight hours of his existence, as he stood on the platform of the station where the ticket expired and the train deposited him, he made the reflection:

"Nine days and nine hundred miles from New York! One hundred miles from St. Louis!" and the nine days seemed nine ages, and the nine hundred miles seemed so many worlds, separating him from the

Benjamin Cleveland he had parted from and the life he had left, in the far east. And for the first time since the commencement of his tramp, he felt alone and lonely.

Tramps! Ben thought he had met many of the brotherhood before, but he now found himself on their great summer range. The solitary free-rider or small detachments of two and three, now swelled to squads numbering so high as a dozen.

In fact he had been dropped by the train on the Great Harvest Route, extending from the wheat fields of Minnesota, diagonally across the State of Iowa, crossing the Mississippi at Davenport, and thence extending clear down into the southern half of Illinois. A strip of country five hundred miles long, that may appropriately be termed the Harvest Range. The herd commences to move northward early in July. Starting in the neighborhood of Du Quoin or Bellville, it follows up the harvest, heading northwest, and ending the summer's incursion during the months of September and October in Minnesota. An eastern person has no conception of the vast army of impecuniosities forming this great herd of harvest tramps. Forth they come from the purlieus of cities, from hospitals, work-houses, poor-houses, soup-houses, and the various charitable asylums that have harbored them during the winter and spring. Up from the orange-scented south; from the pampas of Texas; the stave-timber of Arkansas, the cotton-fields of Mississippi; and from those bon-resorts of the fraternity in the river towns on the Father of Waters — " Pinch " in Memphis, " Under the Hill " in Natchez, " Elephant

Johnnie's " and " Smoke Town " in New Orleans, and other celebrated haunts, where an existence (such as it is) has been dragged through for five months of the year. They crowd the river boats; they haunt the wood-pile landings, they line the tracks and capture the trains on their way to the joys and fattenings of the Harvest Range. Once on the Range and life smiles upon them. Back doors know them so well that during the favored period, the good housewife responds to each knock with a chunk of bread in one hand and a hunk of meat in the other, awaiting no solicitations. And how does the herd graze? They graze off of the charity of a community mellow with the ripeness of harvest-time. There help is needed — they are the monarchs of the hour.

They become despotic. They will not solicit work. Work must solicit them. Their labor is an article in demand, and the price goes up, up, up. There are special rates paid during harvest — paid at no other season. In the years immediately succeeding the war harvest hands received as high as five dollars per day — and were not content. They never are. If wages are two dollars and fifty cents, they demand three dollars. If three they ask for four. It is *their* harvest-time; and without a cent in their pockets and existing on the bread of charity, they will hold out for days together, in idleness, rather than work for less than they demand.

Then a few days work; a glorious spree in which their earnings disappear; and they move off along the Range. As the harvest retreats north they follow it. Neither benefitted in purse or person by the labor they irregularly perform.

The dram shops do a thriving business. Scenes of lawlessness are numerous, and battles with towns that have tired of their arrogant idleness and mendicancy frequently occur. Railroads are blockaded with them. Road employees lead a life of trouble, terror and turmoil. Incidents have been where they have seized trains. They hesitate at nothing. Every year the herd becomes larger, — every year its chance for honest labor smaller and smaller. There is a great enemy eating up their range; destroying their stamping-grounds. It is *invention*. Where seven men held stations and bound in a field, three men on a *harvester* now do the same amount of work. What will you do with the idle four? Where three men labored on a *harvester*, one now drives and the *automatic binder* makes the sheaves. What will you do with the idle two?

"Make producers of them."

Good. Who will make the consumers, were each to produce for himself?

On to the north — to the great grain fields of Minnesota — go the herd. And then they come back again; but no longer the solid army that marched north. Fleeing from the cold they come down in fragments. By boat, raft, and skiff down the great river. By tramping, and jumping the trains. By every conceivable method of travelling they make their way south. Where was this herd twenty-five years ago? We do not know. Like the Texas cattle trade, it is a growth of the present decade.

It was this Harvest Range that Ben now found himself crossing. The herd had left. It was far to the north. Remnants of it were numerous, however. Tramps who had tired of following the trail. Sharp tramps who cutely remained to fatten on the deserted pastures. Sharper tramps who sought the lower rendezvous before the herd returned. Crippled members of the fraternity, left behind. Parties that the law had detained. The stragglers formed quite a respectable army still.

At least our hero thought so, shortly after ensconcing himself in an empty box car on a western bound freight, late that night. It was the only empty and open car in the train, and he was congratulating himself upon holding exclusive possession of it when a gang of four invaded his privacy, and in passing the next three stations the excursionists had augmented to fifteen souls. Of course the train employees became aware of their presence, and ordered them off twice. The first time they all got out and going around to the other side all got in again. On a repetition of the order to dismount they merely laughed and chaffed the conductor. The conductor telegraphed the state of affairs to Maidensville and called for help to eject them. The operator made the dispatch public, and the citizens of Maidensville were apprised of their approaching visitors. The tramps were not blind to these matters. Expecting a forcible ejectment and arrest when they arrived at Maidensville, they guarded against it by refusing to allow the train men to close the doors and lock them in, intending to jump from the train before it drew up at the station. But the engineer threw his valves wide open and ran his train into the depot at a rate that prevented the squad from leaving until it finally stopped. When it did so a surprise awaited all parties. A delegation of citizens was on hand with bread and cheese. It begged the tramps to remain in the car and partake of the food, intimating an immediate arrest for any who dismounted. They were also informed that their ride to St. Louis was paid for, and the conductor discovered to his chagrin, that, by telegraph, the citizens of Maidensville had chartered empty box car No. 1073 to convey a load of live stock from Maidensville to St. Louis — that day and date. The conductor opened his ·eyes. The citizens smiled broadly. And the fair city of Maidensville was relieved from her unwelcome guests.

With much hiliarity the excursionists completed their ride into East St. Louis, where they arrived at noon. But what was Ben's dismay to find a small squad of police ready to receive them as they dismounted! Alas, here he was again, for the second time during his journey, under arrest!

The crowd was taken before the mayor, arranged in a platoon, charged with vagrancy, asked no questions, permitted no defence, found guilty, — and sentenced to sixty days in the work house, and a fine of fifty dollars, each! Good-bye to New Orleans. Good-bye to the twenty thousand dollars. Good-bye to the great, glorious, grey eyes. Our hero was fairly floored. Indignation at this summary treatment was swallowed up in amazement. Struck dumb with the overwhelming nature of his disaster, with drooping head and downcast eyes he followed his companions in misery out of the court room. They traversed several streets, closely attended by policemen, and at last neared the river. The tall chimneys and acres of roofs of smoke-curtained St. Louis arose on the opposite bank. Our friend's heart gave a great leap. There was the city that had filled his mind these many days. There was where he was to have again seen *her*. There was the half-way house of his tramp. Once in it and his journey would have seemed more like an accomplished fact, having attained the first objective point in the stipulations of his wager. And there it was, just across the river — so near and yet so far! A mile of water, sixty days imprisonment, and fifty dollars fine, separating them. Wild thoughts entered his head.

He would break from his captors and rushing to the stream plunge in and swim for the opposite shore. Which, had he done, he might quite possibly have reached New Orleans, but it would have been in a very unenviable state. This desperate notion was forming itself into a determination when his attention was arrested by the voice of the officer in charge of the squad.

"Men," said that official, "yonder's St. Louis, where you all want to go. Remember, if you are caught on this side again, up you go for sixty days. Here are your ferry tickets. Now git!"

It was tit for tat. "Illinois Town" was paying St. Louis in her own currency. That morning the "Future Great" had shipped, by rail, half a dozen of her paupers to Chicago. That afternoon the "Future Great" received a consignment of sixteen tramps from "Illinois Town."

CHAPTER XX.

OUR HERO REACHES ST. LOUIS.

AS Ben placed his foot on the Missouri shore, he cried aloud with an exultant thrill vibrating every fibre of his body : " St. Louis ! Ten days and ten hundred miles from New York ! Hurrah for New Orleans ! " and his emotions were such that he could fairly have turned a double somersault and cracked his heels for joy. Then as his feelings quieted down, " Now for New Orleans," he said. But how ? That was the rub.

The levee was lined with steamboats. Boats with wheels behind them like aquatic wheel-barrows, and boats with wheels at their sides like folded wings. River crafts piled deck upon deck until the pilot-house, perched on top of the " Texas " looked like a birdcage. A forest of black smoke stacks interspersed with golden balls and gilded figures of eagles, horses, cotton-bales, barrels, and various devices. Some of the stacks belching forth smoke like the nostrils of a live monster ; others silent and grim. Light draught stern-wheelers in the Big Muddy trade, that ran way up into the mystic region of the Yellow Stone in the spring and came down in the fall, taking up with them Indian annuities and government supplies, and bringing down bullet-holes in their pilot-houses from the rifles of ungrateful savages who cannot understand why white men should take their land from them and pay them in phantom beeves and unkept treaties. Ohio river tow boats — stern-wheelers also — but aquatic giants. Boats that think nothing of butting their square heads against four solid acres of coal flats, twelve feet deep, and shoving the whole field to the lower river coaling grounds — their very machinery a load sinking them deep in the water, and well worthy of their names, " Ajax," " Hercules," "Colossal," and so on. Raft boats from the St. Croix, Black River and Chippewa, with their holds stowed full of great coils of rope. Trading boats from the Illinois, Tennessee, Arkansas, White and Red Rivers — boats that somehow bore about them a romantic aroma of travel and adventure. Wrecking boats and stump-pullers — that dredge the bottom of the river from St. Louis to the Gulf. Vast floating palaces in the Memphis, Vicksburg, and New Orleans trade — their long, fairy-like and gorgeous cabins elevated on stilts, way high up above the hulls. Boats that could laugh at sixteen hundred tons of freight, and stow five thousand bales of cotton! A solid two miles of these crafts, thick as they could lie, all with their great round blunt noses hanging on the levees.

And then the humanity gathered about them — Diego and African, native and foreigner — people from all over the world. Acres of cotton bales, regiments of hides in bundles, barricades of salt, ramparts of sugar hogsheads; all being constantly added to by a supply from the bowels of the monsters on the levee, while down their capacious maws was poured a stream of flour in barrels, grain in sacks and other productions of the stomach-supplying north. It was a scene of life and activity, such as Ben had never before witnessed. A wonderful picture of commerce proving in stronger tongue than any wordy argument the necessity of an undivided North and South — a UNION!

Ben gazed and wondered, and wondered and gazed, and the more his eyes discovered, the more they sought for; while up against the sky loomed that *chef-d'œuvre* of modern engineering, the famous bridge. He leaned against a cotton-bale and gave his eyes a holiday. And well he might, for the picture has not its equal in all the world.

A light touch on his arm aroused him. He turned and saw — *Tommy!* Little Tommy whom he felt he had known for years, instead of days.

"Ha, ha! I thought I'd find you on the levee sometime," he exclaimed. "All the 'bums' sun themselves here!"

Save that he was a trifle thinner and his round cheek had lost some of its bloom, the boy looked much as he did when Ben parted with him in Harrisburg. The sparkling brown eyes were the same and the ring of his voice had lost none of its silver as he danced around Ben crying:

"Bennie, old boy, I'm awful glad to see you! I am indeed. But how thin you are! Poor Bennie. He'll never make a first class cadjer, so he won't

And, my eyes! How ragged and dirty! Why don't you rent yourself out for a museum of hard times? I hunted, and hunted, and hunted, for you all along the road, but I must have been ahead of you. I came through on express trains, I did. Sometimes on the roof, sometimes on the pilot, sometimes on the platform, and sometimes inside — until I'd get bounced. I made myself bomb-proof with an old shirt and sixteen newspapers, and I'm thinking they hurt their boots more than they hurt me. Laugh again, Bennie. I like to see you laugh — you've got such pretty teeth. And now you're blushing! Oh, Ben, aint you ashamed! There's no use, I may as well give you up for a bad job ; you will never be an ornament to the profession ; never make a first-class war-horse. Now tell me all about where you have been, and how you have been, and — and everything ! " and Tommy quite out of words and wind, stopped exhausted.

Ben was glad to meet a friendly face in the great strange city, and boy though Tommy was, he felt grateful for his friendship.

" But, Tommy, I have not told you all," said our hero after briefly relating his experience on the tramp. " Do you know that I have seen you since you saw me ? "

Tommy looked his surprise and answered :

" No!   Where ? "

" In Pittsburg," and Ben told him how he had stood and listened to the conversation between Black-oat and Nipper, and how Tommy had appeared and disappeared.

Had Ben been more attentive or observant of his

little friend he would have noticed that the hand on his arm trembled, and the boy's cheek paled as he mentioned Blackcoat's name. But he did not, and when he looked up, Tommy's face was a burning red, filled with confusion.

"What a gilly you are, Ben!" he said. "You made a mistake in the dark. It was some one else you saw and could not have been me, for I didn't stop in Pittsburg.

Cleveland looked at him in astonishment.

"Tommy, are you telling me the truth?"

"Truth positive, Benjamin!" With an endorsing nod of the head. "Don't you believe me?"

Ben reflected a moment before he answered, and when he did the words came slow, as though he was trying to persuade himself that he meant what he said.

"Yes, Tommy — I believe you. But I was never before so mistaken in my life. Never in my life."

"It *was* a queer delusion," returned Tom; and there the matter dropped.

"And which way now, friend Ben? You have reached your destination, your pilgrimage is over, there's to be a fatted calf, a purple robe and a gold ring! Is that the programme?"

"No, not quite," answered Ben, smiling. "The fact is my pilgrimage is only half over, Tommy. I am going to New Orleans."

"To New Orleans! Why you told me St. Louis!" cried the boy in surprise.

"Very well, and am I not come to St. Louis?"

"Yes, true enough; but you do not remain here?"

"No, my boy. New Orleans is my destination. I

have some moneyed interests there — if I get there in time. If I don't, — well — the interests are quite as heavy but not of a financial nature."

"All this is a mystery to me, Ben, and I don't ask for your confidence," said Tommy, shrugging his shoulders; "but when is it necessary for you to be in New Orleans?"

"At ten o'clock on the morning of the second of next month; just eleven days from to-day," replied Ben.

"Why you have lots of time! I could go to Mexico by that time," said Tom encouragingly. "I don't care if I take a trip down the river with you, Ben. Which way are you going?"

Ben expressed himself pleased at the prospect of his little friend's company, and thought the river would be their best route.

"So it is, undoubtedly," said Tommy. "You can go from St. Louis to New Orleans for four dollars on deck. Have you four dollars?"

Ben confessed that he had not. That all his cash assets consisted of ten cents, the remnant of the twenty-five he had received from the dray-man in New Jersey City.

"What, you have the dime yet? How saving you are!" cried the other. "But a dime won't take you to New Orleans. Not by river. Say, you fellow, how'll a fellow get to New Orleans?"

This last query was propounded to a picturesque representative of the fraternity who was sunning himself on a neighboring cotton-bale.

"New Orleans? Why buy a railroad and ride

down," replied the party addressed, leisurely turning over on his side, with his face toward our friend's.

"Oh, come, partner, give us a square answer," expostulated Tommy. "We want to get down there."

At this the man sat up on the cotton-bale and requested a chew of tobacco, having obtained which he leisurely continued :

"You can go to New Orleans lots of ways. You can walk down 'long the levees. Lot's of 'em does that. You can beat your way by boat. Lots of 'em does *that*. You can go from here to Cairo by boat or rail and then beat your way from Cairo over the Jackson and Great Northern. Lot's of 'em do *that*. That's the way most of the lake men go down in the fall, and the cotton pickers come up in the spring. The other big north and south road for the bums is the Texas route. And a very good road it is. After you get to Poplar Bluffs — that's the end of the first division — it's clear sailing down to 'Texarkanna. That's a boss town too. Stands half in Texas and half in Arkansas. That's where it got that name. You can shoot a man in Texas and go across the track and be in Arkansas, or wicey wersey, which makes it very convenient for the inhabitants. That road runs catacornered across Arkansas, and its got to be a great cotton route from Texas, which has made it very convenient for tramps."

"Yes, that's all right ; but how about the New Orleans route?" interrupted Tommy, afraid lest the new brother if he continued would get over into Asia and commence barge-lining the Ganges.

"Well, as I was a saying, you can go from here to

Texas, easy as you please, on the Iron Mountain road. I 'spose four thousand tramps go down along it every winter and come up every spring. They're the Texas Rangers of '76 — 1876 ! " and he grinned.

" But is it a good route to New Orleans ? " asked Ben, who was afraid the professional was again about to desert his subject.

"No ; it's a better route to Texas," replied he.

" But we want to go to New Orleans," protested Cleveland.

" Don't you be a fool and go to New Orleans when you can get to Texas," advised their irrelevant informant.

" New Orleans is crowded with tramps every winter. So is all the South, though they don't howl about the matter the way they do up North. You let New Orleans alone. You go to Texas and be a Ranger ! "

" A Ranger ? What sort ? " asked Tommy.

" Range all over the country after handouts," replied the professional with another grin.

" You keep telling us about Texas and we are not going to Texas," said Ben.

" More fool you," placidly commented the Ranger. " Texas is a good state."

Ben was in despair of ever getting information from this source, but made one last effort to obtain it by asking the garrulous professional if they could get to New Orleans by the Iron Mountain road.

" Well, you can and you can't," was the highly unsatisfactory answer. " You can go from here to Little Rock, and can there get off on the Memphis and

Little Rock Road.   That road would take you to the river right opposite Memphis."

" Then it won't take us to New Orleans ? "

" Oh, no.   You'd have to jump a boat from Memphis.   But I say !   Why in thunder don't you jump a boat here ?   That's your best plan.   Jump any of the New Orleans steamers an' keep your eye peeled for the clerk when he comes around.   I see my buddy up the levee.   Good-bye.   Take the boat.   Better go to Texas though.   Might strike a Mexican revolution. Have one every new moon.   Go to Texas.   That's my notion," and shouting back these fragments of advice, the professional withdrew up the levee and was soon lost in the crowd.

" There Tom," said Ben, " we'll have to go by boat."

" I was aware of that long ago," coolly replied Tommy.   " Do you see that big boat down there with the horns on her jack-staff ?   That is the Argenta. She leaves for New Orleans to-morrow afternoon at four o'clock, and you and I will go on her."

This matter definitely arranged the two friends walked up the levee.

CHAPTER XXI.

A SHAVE WHICH HAS A RESULT.

"TOMMY, have you seen any one since you came to St. Louis ?" asked Ben.

" Seen any one ! Why of course — I've seen thousands," replied the boy stopping and looking Ben in the face.

" I mean have you seen any one that I know ?" explained Ben.

" Any one that you know ! That's a singular question. Pray whom do you know ?"

" Come, Tom, you know there is only *one* we both know. Have you seen — *her ?*"

" Her ?" said Tommy obtusely. " Pray now who's *her ?*"

" Be serious, Tom. There is only one *her*, and you know the one I mean. You said I would see them in St. Louis. Are they here ?"

" Oh, *that's* it !" cried Tommy petulantly, and a shade of disappointment crossed his bright face. " You men are such fools ! You never see a pretty face but you must fall in love with it' " and then the boy stopped, and stammered, and blushed, as though in some way he had committed himself.

But Ben was absorbed in his own thoughts and did not notice his companion's confusion.

"Never mind my failings, Tom. Perhaps you will have the same when you get to be a man."

"*Mebbe*," replied Tommy sententiously.

"Tell me then, is the young lady and her companions here?"

Tommy's looks and manner suddenly underwent a startling change. The light-hearted cheerful-faced boy was suddenly transformed into a grave, thoughtful person, and on his countenance was a look of anxiety and even a shadow of hatred, giving his face an expression that startled Ben. After a moment's silence, he replied, with his eyes on the ground:

"Yes, they are here. She is here. You wish to see her?"

"I do, I do," exclaimed Cleveland.

"And for what earthly good or purpose?" petulantly asked Tom.

This caused our hero to stop and look troubled.

. "True," he muttered, "for what end or for what purpose? Would she look at me—*me* a *tramp!* Preposterous! And yet I would like to see her, if only for the pleasure of basking in the glow of those heavenly eyes. For what good or purpose? Who may tell? I have as much right to win her as any one. Pshaw! What an idiot am I!"

And yet he was as sensible as the majority of mankind, and had only been indulging in the pleasant pastime of constructing air castles. Without ties of home or kindred to claim his thoughts during the long days and nights of the tramp, his mind had constantly

reverted to this young woman, and builded in his heart
a creation that had at last taken full occupancy of it.
No wonder then when his daydreams were about to be
brought face to face with reality the practical common-sense of his nature had a hard struggle with the
fascinations of imagination. Tommy observed him
closely and probably understood what was transpiring in his mind.

" Ben," he said, " I have heard that all men are
fools when in love, and I think you must be in love.
That's no concern of mine however, only mind you,
young man, after you have been well scorched, come
to me and I'll tell you something about love ! "

There was such a peculiarly bitter and sarcastic expression in the boy's tone and face that it recalled
Ben's wits from dreamland with a jump and he devoted his attention to his companion.

" Well, rooster, what is it about love that you pro-
fess to know so much ?   Are you in love ? " he asked
with a smile.

" No, but I had a friend once who was," replied
the youth.

" And what became of him ? " asked Ben.

" It wasn't a *him*, it was a ' *she* ' !   And this ' *she* '
fell in love. *Love!* It was something more than
love — it was *worship!* She gave up home, friends,
happiness, *salvation* — everything did she sacrifice on
the altar of her love — and as a natural consequence
she awoke to find the sacrifice rejected."

" And what became of her ? " asked Ben.

" She had her revenge !   She turned dressmaker
and never had her work done when she promised ! "

and Tommy gave a whoop and a shrill laugh. " There
my boy," he continued, patronizingly patting Ben on
the back, " you didn't look for that windup, did you ?
Never mind. When your fair maid rejects you, you
and I'll join hands and tramp all the rest of our lives
together. But I'm a true prophet, Ben ; I told you
you should see those people here, and so you shall.
And now in return for the service I am about to ren-
der you, you must promise that you will ask no questions. Do you promise ? "

Ben promised most faithfully, and the boy con-
tined :

" You shall see her to-day."

" But what is her name, Tommy ? " asked our hero.

" There you go, breaking your promise already.
I'll forgive you this time, only don't do it again. I
don't know her name — at least only her Christian
name. That is Bertha. A woman, to-day, gave me
a note to deliver to her. I am to be on Olive Street,
between Eighth and Ninth this afternoon, at five
o'clock, and hand it to her as she comes along. The
woman gave me ten cents for doing it. I transfer the
duty to you and we will go and dine off of the ten
cents. Come on."

The two friends thereupon dined with the aid of
the ten cents. To be sure it was not an extravagant
repast, consisting simply of two great sheets of gin-
ger-bread, known on the levee as "stage-planks " ;
but keen appetites made them palatable, and with
plenty of water they possessed filling properties to a
remarkable degree.

Ben then turned up Olive Street alone, and as he

walked along the thronged thoroughfare felt, for the
first time during his tramp, thoroughly ashamed of
himself. Could it be that the dirty, ragged, slouch-
ing, unshaved, unkempt reflection he saw in the plate
glass windows, was the Benjamin Cleveland he had
known in other days? Impossible! And yet too
true. The effects of his tramp had altered him won-
derfully.

The elements, combined with coal dust and dirt,
had bronzed his skin. A nine days' growth of beard
stuck out in prickly profusion on his face. The hat,
that had been shapely in New York, resembled a felt
pouch on which an elephant had stepped. His clothes
hung on him strangely. Altogether he hardly recognized himself.

"And she," thought he, "what will *she* think?
I've ten cents and I'll have a shave if it sends me into
bankruptcy, and look a little more human."

When he came out of the barber's hands he certainly did look greatly improved and his clothes seemed
to fit him better.

Having reached Ninth Street he stationed himself
on a corner and awaited the owner of the great, glorious grey eyes. He was looking for two glowing
eyes in a head wrapped up in a snowy nubia.

So it is with us all. Our last remembrance holds
tenaciously upon its pictures; and refuses to surrender them to the march of time and events. After
years have changed the faces and scenes we love, we
return to them expecting to find them the same as
when we left, and feel a dull pain when we find that
our memories of the past belong to the past, and are

not heirs of the present. So Ben stood, gazing down
the street in search of a white nubia, and was fairly
startled into open-mouthed amazement when a voice
nearly opposite to him said :

" Bertha, dear, I am so sorry that you can not remain with us until next week, if not longer. Must
you *positively* go to-morrow ? "

And the person addressed replied :

" I should like to, Mary, but uncle says he positively must go."

The voice of the lady brought 'Ben's senses back,
and there, right before his eyes, was the object of his
worship — more lovely, more beautiful, he thought,
than he had ever pictured her.

Bertha certainly was gifted with good looks far
more generously than her sisters. To be sure she no
longer wore a billowy mass of white worsted about
her head, that Ben's picture was familiar with, but in
its place was a saucy little hat that turned up behind,
and an ostrich feather that turned up in front ; and
at the back of the head and under the cocked-up rim
of the hat was a great roll of chestnut hair, with each
particular hair leading from the snowy neck thereto
drawn as tight and as smooth as the top-hamper of a
man-of-war. Two pretty shell-like ears, that this peculiar mode of hair-dressing made stand out from their
owner's head like a pair of little wings, were kept
from flying away by two diminutive soltaire anchors.
Under the feather and under a broad expanse of snowy
forehead — roofed over by the architecture of the
saucy hat — beamed forth the eyes that had so effect-
ually fastened themselves in Ben's soul. They were

lustrous grey orbs in which the sunlight of high noon seemed to have lost itself. Deep and thoughtful, they were, beaming in purity and confidence; alive with kind promptings, and singing an undying melody of love and faith. Just such eyes as we *do* sometimes see, and ever after remember.

And they lighted up a face worthy to bask in their sunshine. She was dressed richly, but tastefully, with every external evidence of wealth and refinement. Poor Ben's heart sank within him. When now brought face to face with the object of his adoration all his sanguine hopes went down below zero, and the airy castles of his daydreams crumbled to dust. How could he aspire to this elegantly attired and lovely formed mass of femininity! Absurd! He in rags and she in silks! Preposterous! He an unknown *tramp*, she a wealthy belle! Outrageous! He hastily arrived at the conclusion that he was a fool, and immediately called himself one.

CHAPTER XXII.

OFF FOR NEW ORLEANS.

WHILE all this was transpiring, (in Ben's mind) the young ladies had gathered up their trains in one hand, and with the other extended by way of a balancing pole — and because the attitude is supposed to be graceful — were picking their way through the mud of the crossing to the opposite side of the street. The recollection that he had a letter to deliver flashed upon our friend's mind, and he hastily followed them.

" Miss, I am commissioned to deliver this to you," he said, politely lifting the felt pouch from his head.

For a moment it seemed to him that she was about to pass on without taking the missive. Then she appeared to change her mind and asked :

" Who sent it ? "

" It is from a lady, a stranger to me," replied Ben.

" Ah, I understand. Thank you ; " and before Ben knew what had transpired she had taken the note, and from a dainty pocket-book had placed a bright half-dollar in his hand.

When he recovered himself both young ladies were

half a block away, and he staring after them stupidly. That was all. She had not only not recognized him, but scarce observed him at all, and in the little recognition of himself and services that had been bestowed was an air of condescension, and haughtiness of high-breeding, that left the impression in his mind of an utterly impassable gulf between them. Slowly he turned and walked toward the levee, humbled and mortified, and with a singular notion forcing itself in upon his humiliation that his ten cents, expended in a shave, had been money thrown away. His castles had not only tumbled down, but they had buried him in the ruins. For several blocks he crushed the half-dollar in his hand, as though it were the author of his miseries and disappointments. Then, in a moment of wounded pride and passion, he flung it far into the street, and felt better.

" What an ass I am," he said bitterly, " to think that she would have noticed me ! Who or what am I that she should grant me the courtesy of a recognition ? I am an *ass*, that is what I am. And I'll get to New Orleans as quickly as I can, and if I am successful sail from there to Europe, and see if I can't pick up some common-sense over there where all the rest of my countrymen lose what little they have."

" *For Memphis, Vicksburg and New Orleans. The swift and palatial* ' ARGENTA '; SPARBAR, *Master ;* QUILLBUCKER, *Clerk ; will leave St. Louis at* 4 *P. M., to-day. For freight or passage apply on board.*"

The " Argenta " was the pride of the western waters. She it was that ran the celebrated race with the " Chief " there several years ago. Both boats were advertised to go on their usual journey in a quiet, orderly, non-contesting manner. The captains knew nothing about any race. The clerks knew nothing about any race. The mates, engineer, fireman, deck hands and roustabouts knew nothing about any race. Nobody knew any thing about any race. So when the boats backed away from the New Orleans levee out into the broad river there were thousands of persons there to witness their departure and thousands of dollars wagered upon them. Both were stripped to the belt.

Every thing that would catch wind or water was laid aside. Machinery carefully looked to, polished and oiled. Superfluous weights removed and both crafts prepared for the contest that no one knew any thing about. As a result of all this stripping the Argenta came into St. Louis ahead of the Chief, and several thousand sanguine individuals were stripped of their spare change for many months thereafter. It was the " wind up " of Mississippi yachting. A peaceful epilogue to a long drama of bursted boilers, murdered men, scalded deck hands and drowned passengers. Racing on the western waters is out of date and out of fashion.

With deep intonings the Argenta's great bell sounded its final notes of solemn warning. The apple venders and orange peddlers sprang to the shore. The short-card men, fakirs, and magic-knife and thimble-rig manipulators deserted their prey. The huge stage was drawn in and up. The " last man " came rushing down the levee, bag in hand, and was taken on board on a single plank. There was a great jangling of small bells — a moment's silence — and then with a rush and a roar, amid the batter of big paddle-wheels, churning of water, clank of machinery, pulsations of the great exhausts, and the shouts of the crowd on shore, the Argenta backed from her berth into the stream, lay a second or two motionless in the waters, and then turned her nose to the south, and sped for New Orleans!

CHAPTER XXIII.

A NIGHT ON DECK.

BEN sat on a barrel, looking about him in wonder. Fifty negro roustabouts, great sable Hercules they were — scarce half civilized — secured and
arranged the freight and ropes on deck for their trip,
talking the while a mellow-voiced gibberish that he
could but half understand. The mate, as great a
savage as the blacks, though wearing a white skin,
and whose reputation was based upon the fact of his
having killed three roustabouts, directed them something after the fashion of driving cattle. Ben thought
he had a more extensive repertoire of great big round-
cornered oaths than any blasphemy-belching monster
he had ever seen or heard tell of. Our friend wondered the darkies stood the abuse. He thought that
being freemen, brothers and voters they would have
taken umbrage at the aspersions, imprecations and
anathemas hurled at them. He found they rather
liked it, and worked to the tune of the mate's profanity much like a mule team does to the jingling bells
above its hames. Previous to the war a negro was
worth more than a white man. Now a white man is

worth just as much as a black. The war elevated the
white race. To understand this matter the reader
must know that these roustabout crews are not always composed of black men. Some steamers carry
mixed crews — that is white and black men working
together. Previous to the war if a mixed crew were
" up cottoning " the heavy bales gathered from along
the river and an accident occurred, followed by a
splash and the cry " man overboard! " the captain
would anxiously ask, " white or black? " If the answer was " black " the boat was stopped, life preserv-
ers flung overboard, and every exertion made to save
the unfortunate from a stream that swallows up the
strongest swimmer. If " white," however, the captain looked relieved and sang out to the pilot, " All
right! Go ahead! " That was before the war. *Now*
no questions are asked. It is " All right, go ahead,"
any way.

These hard-worked members of the lowest class of
labor in the country (one of the best paid, however)
passed and repassed Ben, piling up the bags of grain,
tier upon tier, until they touched the bottom of the
deck above. On the front of the hull, out in the open
air, stood the battery of boilers, reaching back nearly
to the wheel-house, the few feet of intervening space
on the guards being occupied on the port side by the
kitchen, and on the larboard by the bakery. The
Argenta's culinary department numbering a little army
of thirty persons — cooks, bakers, assistants and
waiters. There were a hundred head of new milch
cows on deck, each side of the battery of boilers,
going south where they would continue to give milk

for two or three years, and then dry up like all cows in the far south. Texas, a state with more cows in it than all the rest of the Union combined, imports her butter and cheese, and does without milk. Back, aft of the wheel-houses, on the guards were a lot of Missouri mules. These with a pet pig that followed the roustabouts around, a few dogs belonging to passengers, and several coops full of noisy chickens and geese made the boat appear to Ben something like Noah's ark. While he was amusing himself in observing these things, Tommy came to him. With his usual business energy Tommy had been looking over the vessel, selecting "stowing" places and informing himself of the clerk's movements.

"We are all safe for below Cairo, any way, Ben," said he. "The clerk don't come around until after the boat leaves there; he's too busy. We won't be in Cairo until to-morrow, so we needn't mind keeping out of the way until then. Let's go back aft and see the fun."

Night had now settled on the waters. Lamps were lit and lanterns hung about the boat. Back aft a scene that Hogarth's pencil would have revelled in, met them. Between the mountain load of grain sacks that occupied the center of the boat and the vessel's stern, was an open space about thirty feet square. In the center of this stood a long sheet-iron stove, and around this stove was gathered a motley crowd of poverty-stricken humanity, roasting potatoes and parching corn, purloined from the sacks. Care, want, dirt, and misery had established themselves on their pinched faces, and the one lantern that hung in the open space giving light to the crowd painted their tatterdemalion coverings with fantastic effect.

"Those are dead-brokes, every one of 'em," said Tommy, "going to try to beat the boat down. We will have lots of company."

Too much, entirely too much, thought Ben. He could have spared some of it. Walking about the narrow limits and seated on bags, boxes, and the floor, were a lot of migrative birds. Sailors from the Lakes, who, having spent their summer on the great "unsalted seas," were now going down to the Gulf to secure berths on "wind-jammers." Laborers, going south in search of work among the compresses and on the levees. Other professional knights of the spade and barrow, bound for the fascination of the "dumps" and the festive "jiggers." There were several of the gentler sex seated around. Not lone-lorn women, but women in collusion with members of the sterner sex who were there. Wives, perhaps. Charitably, perhaps. The yoke of wedlock is not so hard to shift on and off in a certain class of society as it is in that to which the gentle reader belongs, perchance.

The lady voyagers were travelling on various busi- nesses. To "keep shanty" at some levee camp; or pass the winter south with some friends — not exactly a visit of pleasure either. Rather antiquated and a trifle worse for wear they were too. But the gentle- men treated them gallantly. Passed them the circu- lating bottle with a "Drink hearty, miss! It's paid for!" and boiled coffee in pots and oyster cans for them on the stove. Expectorating tobacco-juice and depositing superanuated quids outside the limits of their immediate vicinity, and, in fact, "paid them those thousand and one little attentions which are so grateful to the gentler sex when coming from gentlemen." (The last expression is in quotations on account of not being altogether original.)

There was one female present whom there could be no doubts about, however, even had she not loudly pronounced herself "A high old gal, you bet!" several times, greatly to the edification of the crowd about the stove, and the virtuous indignation of the members of her own sex, who carefully withdrew their skirts from her. This woman, though young and not ill-looking, was a "gun boat" fragment that had drifted off and found herself on board the Argenta.

Gun boats? In every large city there is a portion of the town that visiting officials from other cities are not driven through on aldermanic rides of courtesy. Perhaps the local dignitaries would think it derogatory to have a knowledge of them — perhaps they leave their visitors to hunt up the town for themselves. So have the water-ways of the west a floating life upon them to which we are not anxious to introduce the reader on this trip down the river. The young lady in question circulated among the crowd with a freedom and ease of deportment that astonished Ben.

"It is terrible," said he to Tommy.

"It's disgusting!" replied Tom.

"And yet how many poor lost ones there are who come down this low," continued Cleveland.

And Tommy, growing a little pale, and looking

upon the "fragment" with loathing and pity said
quietly : " Yes, man's victim has no half-way station
on the road to wreck and ruin," and the boy walked
away, to the forward part of the boat, where he sat
down on a coil of rope and gazed fixedly at the black
river.

There was much drinking and subdued carousing
being indulged in. Songs were sung and jigs were
danced, and the crowd seemed determined to inaug-
urate their pilgrimage by a general time of festivities.
The center of attraction, however, was a negro, black
as black could be, who was conducting the fascinating
game of chuck-a-luck in one corner; a cadaverous
countenanced, thin-lipped, hawk-nosed white man act-
ing as banker. The chuck-a-luck bank was not a
very extensive affair, consisting simply of an empty
cracker box mounted on a grain sack, with numerals
from one to six inscribed upon it with chalk. Behind the box the black dealer manipulated the dice,
and at his side the white hawk drew in the nickels
and small change of those in front. Two short stumps
of tallow candles, permanently located in their own
grease, stood on the box and illuminated proceedings.
This scene, peculiar to the river, was a novel one to
Ben. It was full of life and full of vice.

As the night advanced the crowd thinned. Some
went to sleep on the mountain of grain sacks. Others
cleaned up a place on the floor and lay down, while
others went forward and crept under the boilers, for
their warmth. Black and white lay down together.
Ben still watched the scene, which though quieted
down, was still attractive from its novelty. The gun-

boat visitor having satisfied every one that she was a
" High old gal, you bet!" borrowed a nickel from a
susceptible tourist and proceeded to invest in the
chuck-a luck bank. She won, and greeted her success with a shout of triumph that startled the sleepers. But luck soon turned against her and she became peevish, abusive and belligerent; claimed that
the black dealer "fingered" his dice, and suggested
the propriety of dispensing with his services and devoting his body to the flood. She became an annoy-
ance to the game, and the hawk tried to buy her off
with a bribe of two nickels, which she accepted, but
immediately staked them on the ace. The ace lost,
and with a whoop, the damsel sent the box spinning
toward the boiler-deck by a kick, scattering dice, candles, nickels and small change in all directions. In
the crowd of tatterdemalions toasting potatoes, and
parching corn at the stove, were men of action — men
who seize opportunities. The single lantern went out
in a twinkle, and in black darkness, Ben felt a writhing, struggling, kicking mass of humanity on the floor.
Blows, yells, laughter, curses and groans filled the
confined limits of the "deck." A pistol was discharged. Some one cried, "I'm shot!" And the
mate with half a dozen watchmen appeared with lanterns and clubs upon the scene. With the clubs they
untied the human knot on the floor. The gun boat
visitor being dragged from the bottom of the heap in
a sadly demoralized condition, but stoutly clutching a
handful of curly black wool. The tatterdemalions
looked still more tattered, but happy and contented,
as though they had enjoyed themselves. The hawk

and the banker arose bankrupt. All struggled to their feet. No. Not all. One man did not move; not even after the mate kicked him several times. They then rolled him over and pointed out the bullet hole in his head. The man was dead. No one knew who fired the shot, or why. No particular investigation was made. He was a deck passenger, and what are deck passengers? Human live stock — and not a very choice breed either. So they rolled the dead man off to one side and at Cairo he received about fifteen minutes' attention from a coroner's jury, (who made the discovery that he was killed by being shot) and about twenty-five minutes from a jobbing undertaker. The captain of the Argenta paid all expenses rather than have the boat detained, and who the dead man was or where he lived are secrets buried with him.

Ben climbed the mountain of grain sacks in company with Tommy, the two went to sleep immediately under one of the exhaust pipes, where it was warm and comfortable ; for the night air on the river grew quite chilly.

CHAPTER XXIV.

BEN WALKS THE PLANK.

DAYLIGHT found the Argenta at Cairo, where a few thousand more grain sacks were taken on board and the dead man disposed of. At Cairo the vessel also received quite a consignment of tramps, bound South. Tramps coming in off of the great Harvest Range, and tramps from Chicago and the cities by the Lakes. It was preposterous to suppose, for a moment, that the regiment of them now on the steamer could be overlooked by the clerk, or manage to stow out of sight where he could not find them. Still they came, thinking that go so little a distance as they might before being " bounced," it was nevertheless a step in the right direction.

Scarce had the Argenta left Cairo, and before the new travellers had time to familiarize themselves with their surroundings, when the clerk came down on deck and prepared for business. After running everybody back aft, the deck-hands and roustabouts formed a cordon across the boat, between the battery of boilers and the pile of grain sacks, others going to the stern and driving the deck passengers through a gap in the line where the clerk was ready to receive them. When the passengers reached this gap the clerk examined their tickets, or collected the fare where no tickets were produced. When neither tickets nor money were forthcoming, the impecunious were placed in a little group by themselves, under the surveillance of some of the crew. Nothing harsh or unkind was said to them. Indeed their presence there was expected and looked for. Every trip the boat made there were delegations of them on board.

At last the inspection ended. The passengers who had proved themselves all right were allowed to go whithersoever they pleased, and the "bums" were marshalled in a group up forward around the capstan, strictly guarded, and the boat's head turned for Columbus, on the Kentucky shore. Strange to relate, neither of our friends were among either party — the paid or unpaid.

Tommy, with sleeves rolled up and a gunny sack apron on, was washing dishes in the cook's galley, in peace, and security, and — soap suds. How he had accomplished this stragetic movement or ingratiated himself into the esteem of the head cook we do not know — but there the boy was. Ben, on the other hand, was not so pleasantly located. His person was concealed beneath a pile of petticoats! The fact was two of the females in the rear were sitting on our friend's body. During the morning, Ben had struck up quite a friendship with an honest Celt in patched corduroys and hickory shirt. In their conversation it was discovered that the latter had worked an entire summer for Mr. Algernon Smythe, at his Swiss chat-

clet, away back on the sunny banks of Long Island
Sound, when that gentleman was first beautifying his
grounds. Ben adroitly mentioned that he knew Mr.
Smythe, having worked for that gentleman, himself.
A long overhauling of old times ensued, and a bond
of friendship was established. Our friend informed
his new acquaintance that it was an absolute necessity
for him to be in New Orleans on the second to meet
parties with whom he expected steady employment.
Having met with misfortunes he confessed that he was
beating his way, for which his new found friend admired him the more. Now it so happened that this
new acquaintance had established friendly relations
with two of his country-women, deck passengers also.
Two sisters they were, on their way south to meet
their husbands, and keep camp for them on the levee,
while the men worked out a sub-contract. These
ladies being introduced to Ben, and hearing his story,
and their sympathies being enlisted — Ben's personal
appearance speaking loudly in his favor — they kindly
offered, at the suggestion of their gentleman friend,
to sit upon him during the clerk's raid on deck. And
sit upon him they did with perfect success ; not being
required to go forward with the other passengers, but
sending their tickets to the clerk by a deputy. So it
happened that when the Argenta ran her great round
nose up to the bank at Columbus, and the gang of
captured " bums " were put on shore, — the gun boat
visitor among them, loudly protesting that she was
" A high old gal, you bet ! " our friend did not bear
them company.

Whether it was the innate modesty peculiar to the

sex, or whether it was that they thought all danger over, we know not: But this we do know, that Ben becoming somewhat restive under his burden, the younger of the two remarked to her sister, with a blush and a giggle, that she thought he might safely be let up. The elder being comfortably seated, and finding Ben's person a sort of spring cushion was not disposed to move. But our hero giving another twist to his cramped person caused the youngest one to bound up with a low cry, followed by another blush, and Ben emerged to thank the ladies for their kindness. Unhappily, for him, the mud-clerk at that moment came aft. He had about passed Ben when some fatality caused him to turn upon Cleveland and ask him to show his ticket. Ben tried to enter into an explanation ; searched his pockets industriously, and at last, as the clerk became impatient, appealed to his generosity and philanthropy, requesting to be allowed to quietly remain and continue his ride. For an answer the clerk hailed a deck hand and our hero was unceremoniously marched to the bow. The stage had been taken on board and hoisted, and the Argenta was withdrawing her nose from the bank when the mate cried to the pilot " Go slow, a moment! "

" Now, young man, be quick, or you'll go into the river!" This exordium had reference to a stage-plank, (a plank about eighteen inches wide) that, at the mate's direction was stuck out from the guards and weighted on the boat end by four roustabouts — the other end being in the air. Ben was to run out on this plank and jump on shore. He had need to be quick, for with the impetus already received the boat was fast drifting out in the stream and widening the space between herself and the land. With another sharp order to " Git! and git quick!" he ran out on the plank.

Whether it happened by accident or from an inherent love of mischief, hereditary in a direct line from their Darwinian ancestry, we know not, but just then two of the roustabouts altered and fashioned Ben's entire life by teetering each other off of the plank just as our friend was about to spring to the shore from the end of it. The heels of the two other make-weights went into the air while their heads struck the deck with a resonant thump. But Ben! He was gurgling and spluttering in the river, with the stage-plank held in a close embrace.

" Man overboard!" was the cry that brought all of the cabin passengers who were loitering on their deck near the gangway, to the front; among them Captain Sparbar. The mate would probably have allowed Ben to get ashore or go to the bottom, as best he might, but the plank was boat property and worth saving. That worthy, undoubtedly, viewed it as unfortunate that in regaining one he was compelled to save the other, but as Ben hung tenaciously to the plank, both he and it were drawn on board by means of a rope. And there he stood — as wet as the river itself — the very picture of misery.

" Throw the hound on shore!" cried the captain, impatient at the delay. The captain had been both mate and mud-clerk in his day, himself.

" All right, sir!" responded the mate ; and then to the man in the pilot-house: " Hold her nose to the bank a minute, Mr. Hawkins!"

But at this moment a soft female voice was heard saying:

"Oh, don't, captain. See, the poor fellow is nearly drowned. Now as a favor to me, let him remain."

The captain was about to politely protest, when the sweet voice silenced him, and the next moment he called to the mate:

"Let the fellow remain, Mr. Blassfeme!"

Then the bells jingled back by the engineers, and the great boat sprang out into the stream.

Poor Ben, dripping with water, turned his eyes gratefully to the deck above, and there stood the owner of the great, glorious, grey eyes, and by her side stood Blackoat, the captain, and a group of admirers. One glance she gave our hero, and a smile; but the glance bore no recognition, and the smile was for his comical aspect. They were such notices as she might have bestowed upon a persecuted animal, rescued from the hands of its tormentors.

"Shan't I go down and bring your new friend up and give him an introduction, Bertha? He has been washed now, you know," said Blackoat, with a sneer.

"Thank you, Arthur," she replied; "you may thank good fortune that it was not yourself that needed a good word with Captain Sparbar."

"Why, Miss Bertha?" inquired the captain.

"I think I should have let him go on the bank, sir!" and with a ringing laugh, in which all joined but Arthur, she disappeared from Ben's vision.

For a few moments Cleveland stood gazing vacantly at the railing of the upper deck. He half wished that they had left him in the river. Why, he could not reason, but he felt that a greater barrier than ever was now insurmountably raised between the idol of his dreams and himself. Back he went to the battery of boilers, and with many a joke from the dusky fireman dried himself quickly in the hot blast from the fire-doors. This done he sought out Tommy, who having been engaged in scouring dishes in the cook's galley was unaware of what had transpired in front.

After relating his late adventures he said :

" Tommy, do you know who is on board of the boat ? "

" There are a great many people on board of her," cautiously replied Tommy.

" But do you know of any *friends* of *ours ?* "

" No, I know of no *friends* of *ours*," replied the boy sullenly.

" The man that struck you in the street that evening in New Jersey City is here," said Ben.

" Well ? " answered Tom, not at all surprised at the information.

" And — the young lady who was there with him, is here also."

" Very well. What of it ? " asked the lad, vigorously polishing a plate.

" You knew it ? " cried Ben in astonishment.

" To be sure," coolly replied Tommy. " That is why *I* am here."

" Tommy," he continued, after a pause in which he had earnestly examined the face of his companion ; " Tommy, will you answer me a question ? "

" That depends on what the question is," cautiously

replied the other. "What is it you want to know?"

"Are you following this party?"

"See here, Ben, the cook lost his wood-sawyer at that last landing. He was bounced along with the rest of the bums. You are in rare good luck, and have secured a passage clear through to New Orleans. All you want is to make yourself solid on the chuck question. Go speak to the cook right off before any fellow gets ahead of you, and tell him you want to saw wood for your grub this trip. It's a splendid chance!" and Tommy shoved Ben toward the galley.

"But Tom, answer my question first; are you following this party?" persisted our hero, his inquisitiveness proof against the allurements of the wood pile.

Tommy was about to leave him, but changed his mind.

"Ben," he said, "if I answer that question, will you promise never to ask me another concerning them or me so long as we are together?"

"Yes."

"Never; no matter what happens?"

"I'll ask you no more, Tom, for I know it does not concern me; but tell me truly, are you following them?"

"*To the death!*" and the boy's hands clenched and his hazel eyes glittered as he hissed the words. There was such a concentrated hatred and bitterness in the utterance that Ben started back and eyed him aghast.

"There; now you know something that does *not* concern you. I hope you are satisfied. Furthermore the meeting in New Jersey City was no accident. I fol-

lowed them and ran against that — that man with my
hat down, to learn when and where they were going.
Remember your promise, Ben.   Don't trifle with me.
Don't break it.   For I like you Bennie — I — I love
you.   I do indeed, and I don't want to fall out with
you." Saying which, in a voice and manner that had
softened to the tenderness of a girl's, Tom ran into
the galley and resumed the polishing of plates.

Puzzled by the mystery surrounding his little friend,
Ben still remembered his suggestion, and on applying
to the head cook was duly installed as Lord of the
Buck-Saw to his sable Majesty.

Verily hath his lines fallen in pleasant places.   A
rescue from the river, his ride to New Orleans secured,
and here, to cap the climax of his good fortune, here
he was living on the fat of the Argenta's larder, and
only exercise enough to give him an appetite.   New
Orleans and the twenty thousand dollars appeared
already within his grasp.

Two days glided by in peace and plenty. · The du-
ties of his new office were neither irksome nor confin-
ing.   An hour or so's industrial manipulation of the
buck saw provided wood enough to last the cook all
day.   In return for this service, he was called into the
galley and filled to repletion after the other members
of the cook's family were through.   He was the envy
of all the " bums " and deck passengers, passing as a
bloated office-holder among them.   One serious and
matter of fact " dead broke " to whom Ben surrepti-
tiously carried biscuits from the galley earnestly advised him not to do too much at a time, but let each
day provide for itself, so that in case the boat blew up

or sunk he would not be a loser. Indeed Ben grafted happy moments on the lives of many poor devils by secreting victuals about his person while in the galley and distributing them among the more starved of the free-riders. There were still a goodly number on board and every raid of the clerk landed three or four. Where they managed to stow themselves so as to escape observation was a mystery to him.

CHAPTER XXV.

OUR HERO TAKES A SWIM.

MEMPHIS was passed and numerous points of historical interest. Points that had dyed the river crimson in the days gone by. But the river shows no stain — let us sincerely hope the country does not. The Argenta had passed Napoleon early in the evening. Napoleon is situated in Arkansas — that is in the aqueous part of that commonwealth — for Napoleon lies at the bottom of the river. Some years ago the stream made a highwater dinner off of several plantations and then ate up Napoleon by way of desert.

It was a lovely starlit night, and the soft, balmy air of the southern country had a soothing lullaby in it, that entranced our travellers as they lounged at full length on the guards of the port side. Ben lay with his elbow on a pile of ropes and his head resting on his hand. Tommy had nestled close to him and was softly humming a tune, all to himself. On the deck above was heard the murmur of voices and ripples of laughter proceeding from the cabin passengers, as they also sat out enjoying the evening. Suddenly a rich soprano voice broke out in Foster's lovely melody, " Way down upon the Swannee River," and the notes went floating over the waters, and way off to the dark line of timber that skirted the horizon of their vision.   In the chorus there mingled fine tenor and bass voices.   Ben lay entranced.   He recognized his infatuation from the first note.   He listened for a verse or two and then unconsciously joined in the refrain himself:

> " All the world is sad and dreary,
>   Every where I roam ;
>   Oh, darkies, how — "

The song was never finished.   There was a harsh, groaning, crunching noise ; the boat quivered from stem to stern and lurched over like a drunken man ; a crashing of timbers followed ; and Ben found him-· self hurled far out into the river.   Even in his transit through the air he heard the cries of alarm and shouts of fear that rent the stillness of the night. Then the great river embraced him, and he commenced battling for life.   Down, down he sank, and when he rose to the surface, his head struck against a plank and he seized upon it, and found to his joy that it would just about support his full weight.   For an instant the glare from the open fires of the boilers shot a broad avenue of light over the waters, and there in the center of the illuminated pathway, there flashed from darkness into light and from light into darkness again, the face of Tommy as he clung to one end of a spar while at the other extremity was Blackoat, his countenance ghastly with a supernatural terror that something worse than the fear of death had produced.

It was but a moment that they were in view and then the current had swept them into the gloom. But the light had revealed another form to Ben. A form that had turned a beseeching face toward him from the cruel waters, and then sank beneath them. The next instant he felt his limbs grasped from below, and reaching down a hand to release himself it became tangled in the meshes of a woman's hair. With an effort he raised the body, and there in the cold star-light was the countenance of Bertha facing him! A thrill of joy even in that terrible moment shot through his frame. He tried to draw her semi-insensible form upon the plank, but found that it sank beneath their united weights. With an arm over the plank he slid into the water, and after much exertion managed to get her upon the preserver he had deserted. It not only bore her weight, but allowed him to hang upon it with his hands, and partially kept him up. Ben was a good swimmer and with this support had a chance for life. But the Argenta, their only hope of rescue, where was she? Afar off — it appeared to Ben miles away — her cabin lights were seen on the waters; and another light moving about in her near vicinity that Ben surmised must be the steamer's yawl boat searching for those thrown overboard.

Would they find him? Could they hear him? Every moment the distance between rescue and him-self was growing greater and greater. He shouted with all his strength. Again and again he called for help! Alas! The river and the night swallowed up his cries. The plank with its precious freight drifted swiftly away from succor.

The causes leading to Cleveland's shipwreck are briefly told. The Argenta was hugging a point on the left bank, and just as she had made it and was about to shoot for the opposite bend, a long, slimy snag caught in her larboard guard and went crashing through to her " Texas," scattering to right and left everything in its course, and throwing our two friends, and the party of cabin passengers, sitting on the deck above them, into the river. The headway of the boat tore her loose from the snag with a loss of guards and decking, but no serious injury to the craft's hull, and the motion she was under carried her far out into the stream before the engines could be reversed and her headway checked. When she at last controlled herself the victims of the disaster were being rapidly swept away, out of hearing and reach, by the point current. The steamer's boat picked up one man clinging to the end of a spar. His face was ashy, his eyes wild, and his mouth set agape with a speechless terror. When spoken to he did not answer, and they were compelled to drag him forcibly from the spar into the yawl. Fright had evidently overthrown reason, and he remained in this dumb terrified state long after the steamboat was regained.

It was Blackoat.

He was the only one found. The Argenta steamed up and down and across the river in every direction. But in vain. The flood surrendered no more, and at last the captain was compelled to relinquish his search and the vessel's head turned toward its destination.

But how fared our voyagers on the plank ? Ben saw the Argenta's lights grow fainter and fainter with a sickening feeling of despair, and when at last they faded entirely from view and he was left alone on the face of the cruel flood his heart sank within him. Like many another shipwrecked person he might have lost strength when he lost heart, and quietly surrendered himself to the remorseless waters. He might have done so, and whispered to himself as he relinquished life: "It's not worth an exertion," as perhaps men have done before him. But there on the plank, by which he buoyed himself, lay his whole world. Life was dearer and sweeter to him at that moment than ever before. His eyes tried to pierce the gloom that surrounded them and discover a shore that he might point the plank with its precious burden toward. But the starlight gave him no aid. All was black and dark. An impenetrable gloom enshrouded them. He had managed to arrange the young woman's person on the plank so that it upheld her in safety, and to make assurance doubly sure he took a scarf that was pinned about her shoulders and bound her to the board while he trod water.

"Should I get cramped and go under, she may float to some landing," he thought.

For half an hour this strange voyage continued in silence, the swift river's current drifting them along at a rapid speed. Then the form on the plank gave evidence of returning consciousness and Bertha murmured:

"For heaven's sake, where am I?"

"There has been an accident. You and I are floating on the river. Be calm. Cling to the plank. We are all right. We will drift on shore or be picked up. Be of good heart."

"Oh, will you save me, will you save me? I don't want to drown — I can't die so! Oh, will you try and save me?" and in her fright she clutched Ben's shoulder.

"Yes, yes, I will save you — or die attempting to. Compose yourself," replied Ben, earnestly. "There is no immediate danger so long as you keep the plank. Don't hang on to me so, please, or I will go under."

The girl withdrew her hand and laying her cold wet cheek against his, he having his chin resting on the plank, she murmured:

"You will save me, I know you will. You are so good. Don't let me drown, will you?"

"No," answered Ben, stoutly; "you shall not drown. We will drift somewhere soon where we can be rescued. You shall be saved, fear not. Have confidence in me, my darling, for I love you!"

"I will, I do. I *know* that you will save me," she earnestly replied.

On, on drifted this young couple through the darkness. Now she would pray, long and earnestly, and Ben would say amen. Then she would beg him not to desert her, and he would valiantly protest that his life was at her service. Between prayer and supplications they got tolerably well acquainted. She promised the love and gratitude of a life time, and he vowed that to save her life at a sacrifice of his own would be charming.

Though treading on the tail of Death's coat, strange to say, Ben was happy. He caressed her, as well as circumstances would permit, and now and then kissed her hand and even her cheek, which she did not

withdraw from him, but would arouse herself and ask :
" Are we near the shore ?   Do you see the shore
yet ? "

" Not yet ; not quite.   Be of good heart," he would
reply.

Then a silence would follow, broken again by her
pleadings : " Are we near the shore ?   Do you see the
shore ? "

So several long dreary hours wore by.

" Are we near the shore ? "   Do you see the
shore ? "

And Ben's voice grew weaker and weaker, and his
answers slower and slower, when he replied to her
supplications :

" Yes, yes, dear ; near the shore.   Near the shore,
I pray God," for there was a dead faintness and a loss
of energy coming over him.

He was growing exhausted and several times his
hold upon the plank grew so heavy that it sank deep
in the water ; at which Bertha would cry out that
she was drowning and call piteously upon him to save
her.   Then mastering himself, for a time our hero
would strive to float without hanging to the board,
but each attempt grew shorter than the preceding one,
and he felt himself swiftly drifting into Eternity.
Once his hold on the plank loosened and he began to
sink.   A spasmodic effort regained his buoy, but his
grasp caused it to sink, and with a shriek the maiden
implored him to save her !   Her voice aroused his
drooping energies, and gave him new strength.   But
presently it faded away, and death closed in upon him.

" Are we near the shore ? "

"I hope so — I pray God so," said Ben in a weak voice. " Will you — will you kiss me — just once ? "

She would have kissed him a thousand times had it been possible.

" Thank you. God bless you, and save and protect you, darling. Cling tight to the plank. For I feel myself going ; —I — I — can't hold out, — no, not much longer. Don't — let go — good-bye ; — I — I always loved you. Good. Don't let go. Hang tight. Good —. What ! Thank God ! Thank God ! We are saved ! Saved ! Saved ! Bertha we are saved ! My feet touch the bottom ! I can *walk !* "

It was indeed a joyful fact and one that was much needed at that identical moment. A few seconds later and Ben would have been too weak to keep his feet. But now a new life and a new strength was given him.

" Wait ; I will see if this is the shore," he said. Then with his face close to the water he peered around him.

" I cannot tell," he presently said. " There is a dark line to the right and I will make for it. Hold tight to the plank for should I step into deep water you will need it."

Slowly pushing the plank in front of him he made his way toward the dark line he had taken for the shore. For several minutes he cautiously waded through the flood, and the water fell from his chin to his breast and from his breast to his thighs and then he could see land ahead of him with bushes on it. At this happy discovery he set up a great cry of joy, and unlashing Bertha from the plank, took her in his arms and floundered through the shallow water to the shore. And when they reached it they both went on their knees, and prayed such a prayer of thanksgiving, with such heartfelt earnestness, that we are sorry to reflect that it requires such severe causes to produce such commendable effects.

Ben arose from his knees first and stood looking upon his beautiful companion. When she had completed her offering, she arose also, and taking both of Ben's hands in both of hers, she kissed them passionately.

" You saved my life," she said, " and I will never, *never* forget it."

The words were music in his ears, but he modestly protested that the services he had rendered were his duty, and nothing more.

"No! No!" she exclaimed. "You and I have been too near death's door to hold any reserve between us. You saved my life, and to my dying day I will love you for it, and pray to my God that he will reward your courage and goodness."

Ben actually thought then and there that it was worth a dozen wrecks, and a score of close calls from the Great Reaper to earn such a reward.

" I was fortunate in having the opportunity to do you a service," he gallantly replied; " pray do not again mention it. I suppose there are houses in the vicinity, and if you will wait here I will make a search for a road."

" No, rather let me go with you. It is so lonely here and I am chilled;" and the unfortunate young lady's teeth chattered in verification of the last statement.

In spite of her protests, Ben took off his coat, and wringing the water out of it as thoroughly as he could, wrapped it around his fair companion's shoulders. Then confidingly nestling her hand in his the castaways started on a voyage of discovery.

CHAPTER XXVI.

THE CASTAWAYS.

THEIR walk was not a long one. Forcing themselves through a thicket of young cottonwoods, that scarce reached above Ben's head, a few rods brought them to water on the opposite side.

" It must be a point," said Ben ; " a neck of land jutting out into the river. Let us follow it up."

So hand in hand, like two full grown babes in the woods, they walked down the sand that skirted the cottonwood brake. In less than half a mile they came to the end of the brake, and a rod farther brought them again to water. Ben stood speechless. Slowly he turned to his companion, whose wistful, confiding gaze nearly unmanned him.

" Bertha," at last he said, huskily, " we are on an island."

Bertha hid her face in her hands and bowed down in grief at this dire information.

" Don't cry," said Ben simply and soothingly, and, it must be confessed, wrapping his arms about her drooping form, and soothing her head on his bosom as gently as a mother could have caressed it. " Don't

cry. The Hand that brought us here can take us off
again. The river has spared us; fear not but we will
get off of the island safely."

And with many gentle endearments and soothing
speeches he restored her.

"You are shivering with the cold, Miss Bertha,"
he said.

"I am cold, very cold, dear friend," she replied;
"but so are you. Think of yourself. Put on your
coat again. Morning cannot be far off, and then the
sun will dry and warm us."

But Ben refused the coat, and knew that morning
was some hours distant, and that the coldest portion
of the night was yet to come upon them, before the
sun arose and warmed all nature back to life. So he
drew Bertha into the centre of the cottonwood brake,
that protected them from the night breeze now keenly
felt sweeping down the river. Then he prepared a
bed out of twigs and leaves, and bidding her lie down
he spread his coat over her and piled leaves and
boughs high up around her. Ere long his labors were
rewarded by hearing her draw the deep, regular
breath of slumber. Then he laid down beside her,
and exhausted nature courted sleep, despite the shiv-
erings of his cold wet body.

When our hero awoke the sun was shining down
upon him from a cloudless sky. There were also
shining upon him two great, glorious, grey eyes, as
Bertha sat a short distance away, contemplating him
sadly. He noticed with a thrill of pleasure that she
had carefully covered him with the coat, and heaped
the twigs and boughs, that had formed her own bed,

about him. The young lady must have been awake
some time, for with the instinct predominant in her
sex, she had made some futile attempts at a toilet.
Her dishevelled and sand-ladened hair was coiled in a
mass of not unpleasing snarls, and over it she had
tied her dainty lace handkerchief, having had no hat
on her head at the time of the catastrophe. The
drapery of her rich dress was sadly creased and
wrinkled, and she wore all the appearance of a young
lady that had taken an involuntary bath, and then
been only partially wrung out. A memory of the
array of good taste, wealth and fashion that passed
him on Olive Street, in St. Louis, flitted through
Ben's mind, and in spite of himself he smiled at the
contrast. She evidently understood what was upper-
most in his mind, for returning smile for smile, she
said :

" My experience on the river has not been conducive to good appearances. You must be gentle in
your criticisms."

But Ben vowed she never had looked so lovely in
all her life. Which, indeed, she had not ; for there
was a touching grace in the way she bore her distress
that enhanced the charms of a naturally beautiful
woman.

" Your clothes are not dry," said Ben.

" Not quite," she replied, " but I think they soon
will be." A look of misery crossed her face as she
said so, however, plainly indicating that the wet sand-
ladened garments she had slept in, and which were
now clinging to her person were anything but congenial to physical comfort.

"Remain here for a few moments while I take a look at our island and discover some means of escape from it, if possible," said Ben.

It did not take him long to become familiar with the topography of his new location. It was simply a sand bar half a mile long, and from four to five rods broad, standing in the middle of an old channel. The centre of the bar was but two or three feet above the river's surface, but was already covered with that dense and rapid cottonwood growth peculiar to the river country of the south. Off to the west, half a mile away, was another, but a much longer island, also covered with small trees. On the east a deep, swift channel separated the castaways from a wide expanse of the everlasting cottonwood brakes that stretched a mile inland and appeared joined in the back ground to a heavy forest. To the north and south two points of land, heavily timbered, ran far out into the river and closed up the horizon.

Ignorant as Ben was of the shifting nature of the Mississippi, he could easily surmise that in no distant past the river had swept around the point above him and formed the bay in which his island, and the other stretches of sand flats, lay.

It was not *then* a bay, but a bend. Then there had come a change. Perhaps it was a " wash-out" miles up the river, or a caving of bank nearer at hand. Or perchance a farmer in scouring his plow ran it through some narrow neck of sand, miles away, and the river had made its bed in the furrow, leaving whole townships inland, and putting other whole townships to soak. Whatever the cause of it, the current had evidently at a comparatively recent date been shot straight out from the point, instead of circling around it. The deep bay had filled with sand and cotton-wood timber sprouted upon it. Left to itself a century and the cottonwoods on the sandbar would have grown to great trees, and been thrown to earth by the stronger arms and more powerful growth of oak, ash, and sycamore. Another century and the oak, ash, and sycamore would have bowed to the woodman's axe. The plow would have turned up their foothold. Broad acres, rich with cotton and corn, would have flourished on the captured domain. A "corner" grocery would have started. Then another, and another, and another. First a hamlet, then a borough, then a city. Then the iron horse would make his way in the young metropolis, and it would grow with a wondrous' growth. Mayors, and churches, and rings, and subsidies, and aldermen, and defaulters, and debts, and boards-of-trade, and societies, and "bosses," and — all the paraphernalia that goes to make up a great city, would be grown on that sandbar where Ben stood.

But these things were not to be. There had been another "wash-out," another cave-in, or another plow furrow, somewhere else, and the river was slowly coming back to its first love, and if no "wash-outs" or furrows intervened the island Ben stood upon would in a few years again be the river's channel.

Although all of this was not surmised by him he saw enough to fill his mind with dark forebodings. He knew no boats would come that way, for even as he looked a steamer's smoke curled over the point of woodland, miles to the north of him, and disappeared without ever once allowing him to catch a glimpse of the vessel it issued from. The land side was evidently as uninhabited as the long island on the west, and both separated him in their lonely barrenness from succor. Had they then been rescued from the river only to die a lingering death of starvation and exposures! Not a match to light a fire with. Not a stranded log to float from their island prison upon. Their rescuing plank drifted off. Not strength enough to breast three yards of the swift current that swept by them. Nothing but to face fate, and — *die!* The position was horrible. Had he been by himself he thought he could have borne its terrors composedly. Nay, he was no coward, and when the worst came to the worst and he was no longer able to bear the pangs of hunger and the miseries of loneliness, he could have consigned his body to the river without a shudder. But to see her, the idol of his existence, the woman he adored, perish inch by inch, moment by moment, and not be able to extend a single aid — *that* made his heart tremble. Slowly and with down cast eyes he made his way back to where Bertha sat.

" Well," she said, greeting him with a smile, " is this Crusoe land ? "

For a moment he thought of hiding the real facts of the case, but on reflecting that she must shortly discover them herself, he made known their deplor- able position to her. Before the recital was over she was weeping bitterly.

" Don't, don't, please don't, Miss Bertha," said Ben, piteously. " You quite unman me. It may not be

so bad after all. Some boat might come this way, or
we may be able to make our presence known to those
who can rescue us. While there is life there is hope.
The Hand that drew us hither, will not leave us here
to perish, be assured."

Bertha arose and placing both hands on his breast
looked him mournfully in the face, as she controlled
her feelings, and said :

" I have confidence in Him, my good friend, and if
I give way to weakness you must remember the
dreadful trials we have passed through ; nay, that we
are *now* passing through, and that have made me
physically weak, and oh! —" and the lips quivered
and the grey eyes again filled with tears ; " I — I feel
so wretched !"

Now by all authorities — that is, written authorities, — Benjamin Cleveland should have drawn himself apart from the innocent being fate had cast him
alone upon this island sand bar with, and been too high-
minded to take advantage of circumstances. He
should have occupied a high moral plane, in which
even a platonic passion would have found no existence,
and consoled her with dull platitudes and stilted
phraseology. They all do it that way — in the nov-
els. Alas, Ben did nothing of the sort. He acted
on impulse. He wound his arms about the fair form
and pressed it close to his breast, and as she pillowed
her head on his shoulder he kissed her hair, her forehead, her cheeks times innumerable. And she liked
it ; she felt better ! !

He said not a word, for he had nothing to say, but
he petted her like a mother would her child, until her

drooping spirits revived and she smiled at his endeavors in her behalf. From his own condition he readily appreciated the feelings of his companion. There was a growling, discontented vacuum loud in its demands to be filled; that sick, weak feeling of hunger that succeeds exertion and exposure. They were both hungry — very hungry; for hunger makes louder demands at the commencement of privations than it does after time has allowed the muscles of the system to contract and close with a tight grip upon starvation's emptiness. Added to their unappeased appetites, was the miserable, creeping, disgusting feeling occasioned by wet clothes filled with irritating sand. These are humble details, we will admit; but they were the gigantic realities of the moment to the castaways. Ben realized the facts and actively engaged his mind in search of a remedy.

"Miss Bertha," he said, "let us at least make ourselves as comfortable as circumstances will permit. These wet and stiffening clothes, filled with river sand, are unbearable. Listen to me. I will go to the other end of the island and wash the sand out of mine, and do you remain here on the sunny end and do the same. Hang them on the cottonwood bushes until they are thoroughly dry, and keep yourself in the warm sunshine. Exercise too — run, jump, or do what you please so as to keep the blood in circulation; it is positively necessary for us to do all in our power to court health and comfort, or we will sink down under exposure. I will not be back for two hours."

In her loneliness she was loth to part with him at all, but he said reassuringly:

" I will be within hail, and as there is not a living thing on the island, you need not fear intrusion," and then kissing her tenderly, (for he had got into that pleasant fashion and his caresses had never yet so much as brought the faintest blush to her cheek — or his) Ben walked to the upper end of the sand bar, behind the cottonwoods, and there disrobed.

While seated on the sand, his wardrobe adorning the neighboring bushes, he reflected on the gravity of their position.

CHAPTER XXVII.

CRUSOE LIFE.

AS has been stated, the smoke of a steamboat had been seen at the point above, without the boat coming in view, and during the forenoon another went by opposite. He could hear the beat of her paddles, and see the long, thin line of smoke hanging in the heavens over beyond the low island in the west. But the vessel never came in sight. Evidently the main current set across from the point to a bend, probably miles away, in the opposite shore, and boats going down stream took the current, while those coming up hugged the bend to avoid it. Quite likely the nearest the passing crafts came to the castaways was the point above, at least three miles to the north. It was plainly evident that they could not make their presence known to these.

Once while seated on the sands he thought he heard the faint echo of hounds, baying in the dark grey timbers that stood bold against the sky in the east. But what of that? There was a long cottonwood sand flat between his island's channel and the timbers, and who could tell the number of other channels and deep lagoons that intervened before the timbers were reached ? The more he reflected upon the matter the more was he convinced that an escape from the sandbar depended entirely upon their own exertions, and sincerely regretted that he had allowed the plank to drift away the previous night.

What was to be done ? That was the momentous question; for whatever was to be done, would have to be done quickly, while strength lasted. All Ben's latent ingenuity was taxed for relief — stimulated by the cravings of his empty stomach. At last he struck upon the following plan, — the only one appearing feasible or practicable. The cottonwood brake that covered the bar, was of two or three years' growth, with the shoots as thick as a man's wrist at the butts, and standing seven or eight feet high. Rather slender poles to use, but with his pocket-knife and the help of Bertha he hoped to get enough of them together to make a raft that would bear their united weights. He knew it would take a large number, but it was their only hope, and they could continue piling tier upon tier, until they made a serviceable float. When their raft could bear them, he would await a favorable breeze from the west, and with a skirt of his coat for a sail, take to the current and try to make the wooded point four or five miles below. Should they miss a landing, there was the open river to be gained, and a chance of being picked up by some boat, while where they were none but Death would come to the rescue.

The sun had mounted to meridian and was on its way to the western horizon before Ben's clothes were dry. In the interim he employed himself in building a hut out of the cottonwoods. ·With his hands he scraped a hole a foot deep and four feet square in the sandy soil of the brake. Around this he propped up a thick wall of the young trees and covered it with a roof of the same. After placing a heavy carpet of twigs and leaves on the floor, the hut was comparatively comfortable. It would give them a shelter during the day and protect them from the river breeze at night. He now dressed himself, and noticed for the first time an alteration in his person, a sooner discovery of which would have afforded him much comfort. His skin had grown red as a boiled lobster and was painfully sensitive the moment his clothes touched it. While the sun had been drying his clothes it had been baking him. Despite the pain he remembered with a pang of remorseful apprehension the advice he had given Bertha, and was filled with alarm lest she had literally obeyed him, and was now in a similar predicament — only worse.

When they met he cautiously advanced the matter by delicately intimating his own broiled condition, and apologetically inquiring as to her state. But Bertha only laughed and said, " What an idea ! " from which he inferred that his unfortunate advice had not been religiously observed.

Then the young couple walked to their new house.

" We will go to housekeeping here," said Ben, pleasantly ; and Bertha blushed, that time.

Both evidently felt much improved in their dry clothes, and though ravenously hungry, the first pangs of emptiness had modified themselves.

" We will have to issue cards," continued our hero merrily. " At home, September 26th, Mr. and Mrs. Benjamin Cleveland, *nee* Bertha ——," and there he suddenly stopped.

" My name is Ford," said Bertha quietly, though not unpleased at her companion's facetiousness. " Bertha Ford, and I infer from what I have just heard that I may address you as Mr. Benjamin Cleveland ? "

" No, indeed, you may not," exclaimed Ben, warmly. " You must call me ' Ben.' I have earned that privilege, have I not ? "

" Indeed, indeed I'll call you any thing you wish — *dear* Ben if you want me to ; for did you not save my life ! " and with two soft, white little hands in his, she looked so winsomely grateful into his face that Ben blushed in ecstasy, — stammered — and said — he knew not what.

At all events it was arranged that they should call each other by their Christian names, and this dangerous precedent established, there is no telling how far circumstances and surroundings might have carried their intimacy, was it not that on the one side there was the bright honor of a first and picturesque love, that would no more have allowed an evil thought to sully it, than it would have permitted an injury to be done to the object of its adoration ; and on the maiden's part were innocence and purity — needing no bulwarks and for which twin virtues the conventionalities of society were never builded.

Having examined the hut Ben told her of his plan to escape, and she flushed with hope and was anxious to commence the work immediately. So at it the two went. He cut down the young trees and she carried them in armfuls down to the water's edge, where it was proposed to build the raft. When night overtook their labors, quite a pile of the cottonwoods had been accumulated on the strand to reward their industry. Ben's hands were blistered and Bertha's arms were tired and sore, but both felt the elasticity of hope. During the early part of the afternoon's labors much laughter was occasioned at the young lady's appearance. To see a very pretty young woman with white jewelled hands and diamond-draped ears packing brushwood through the sand, the long heavy trail of a rich dress sweeping behind her, was ludicrous. After sweeping a few furrows, Bertha came after her load without the trail, and things progressed better. They said but little, and what was said was only to encourage each other at their labors.

As it grew chilly with the evening breeze sweeping down the river they retired to the protection of the hut, and there (though it was no doubt highly indecorous) seated on the carpet of boughs the head of Bertha found Ben's shoulder and his own stout arms wound about her form. Ben afterward stated that had it not been for the fact of his being everlastingly hungry, he would consider it the happiest moment of all his life.

" Ben ! " suddenly said the young lady.

" What is it, Bertha ? " he asked.

" Do you know it seems to me as though I had known you for ages, instead of for only a single day. Is it not strange ? "

Now Ben did not think this so very strange. He had no cogitation with himself about the fellowship of misery, but he did know that during the entire afternoon when she came up from the strand after her load of trees and he had freighted her with them, they had looked into one another's eyes in a confidential manner that had deeply impressed him. And sometimes when his cuttings had not accumulated fast enough to furnish a load, she had stood by his side and in a soft, caressing way had patted his back and shoulders encouragingly, and when he looked up there was a smile on her lips and a great wide eyed look of confidence and gratitude beaming down upon him. When their eyes met they spoke — not in a language of vowel sounds and consonants, (which same vowels and consonants when they have an opportunity of materializing rush and tumble over one another, and cram themselves in where there is no earthly use for them) they spoke not by breath shaped into philological mysteries, but in the old, old tongue, that has been spoken since Adam first held converse with Eve, and several years before that event, perhaps.

" Does it seem strange to you, Bertha ? It don't to me. I feel as if I had known you always — and that I will know you forever ! "

Bertha was silent.

"Do you hear me, Bertha —*forever !* "

" Bertha, *I love you!* I love you dearly and truly. I love you — ! "

Before he could finish Bertha had withdrawn from his arms, and now sat a little apart, trying to look kindly into his face through the darkness, and holding both of his hands in hers.

"Ben, *dear* Ben, don't love me *that* way," she simply said. "Love me as a sister. Love me as a very, *very* dear friend, but do not think of a nearer or closer relationship, Ben. I know I owe my life to you, and I would gladly do any thing for you that lay in my power ; *love you,* — I do, *I do!* So dearly that I would die for you. But Ben — I can not marry you. I am to be the wife of another. *It is settled!*"

There was a sorrowful cadence in the last three words that made Ben forget his own misery in compassion for his gentle companion.

"*Settled*, Bertha! Do you *love* him?" he asked, not just at that moment reflecting that it was none of his business, and that the question was an impertinance and an insult.

But instead of answering his question, she said with tears in her voice :

"Listen, my kind, dear friend, while I tell you the little there is to my life. I was born eighteen years ago. When but little more than four years old my father died, leaving my mother in straitened circumstances with two children ; myself and a little baby sister. Ben — " and she softly placed a hand on his arm, "that little sister has never risen from her bed. She is now fourteen years old, and all those fourteen years have been spent in patient suffering.

"When I had grown to be quite a girl, a bachelor uncle, my mother's brother, adopted me, and all the advantages that wealth could offer I had. Two years ago this uncle died leaving a singular will. His property, amounting to some three hundred thousand dollars, must remain undivided, and yet he wished it shared between a nephew and myself. To accomplish this the will directs that I am to marry my cousin within two months after attaining the age of eighteen. In case either refuses to enter into the alliance, the entire estate is to go to the one agreeing to it — the other to be left unnoticed. Or in case of either marrying other persons than those specified in the will the property goes to the one remaining single. Should both marry, the property is to be divided up among a number of charities. Both my cousin and myself have employed able legal talent, but they all agree that the will is drawn up in a manner that absolutely prevents any other disposition of the property, than those specified. My dear friend, I have a darling mother who has seen many hardships and trials; one who has loved and watched over me, and sacrificed and suffered for me as only a mother can. I have a poor, helpless, little sister — bed-ridden for life. The income I now receive from my share of my uncle's property provides them with a comfortable home, and furnishes those necessities, both little and great, without which life, under the best of circumstances, is hard. How much more then would it be for a poor helpless little invalid? Tell me Ben — tell me my good friend — have I a *right* to refuse my cousin's proffered hand? Have I a right to take from those two dear ones the only support they have? *Is* my life or person my own? Tell me, you who are so noble and brave; you who would have given up your life for me — tell me, am I right? For, Ben, I feel that I owe my life to you, and would now be a corpse at the bottom of the cruel waters if you had not freely risked your own existence for mine. I *feel* this, and feeling it I give myself to you ; it is the least return I can make. You have heard my story; you know my position; would you have me break my engagement ? "

Poor Ben! Alas, poor Ben! Stone by stone the temple had gone up. Column, and coigne, and architrave ; tower, and entablature, and dome. And here lay the fairy castle — all tumbled at his feet! Built of air, and into air it had vanished. Bad, black, selfish thoughts strolled over the ruins. Every one for himself. What should he care for a mother he had never seen, and a sick sister he did not know ? What were their ease and comfort to him. The girl by his side had confessed that she loved him. True the confession may have emanated from an overwhelming sense of gratitude that subverted all other responsibilities. But what of that ? Evidently from the plenitude of her heart and innocence she felt as she had spoken — that he had saved her life, and that it was *his*. Why should he not claim it ?

Poor Ben. It was so hard to see his castles tumbled down. So hard to find his daydreams so near a realization and then to give her up. He *could* not, he would not. Not until that moment did he know how completely this love had taken possession of him. Day by day, hour by hour, minute by minute, during all the long miles of his tramp it had been subtly permeating every sense of his body. And must he now pluck it out ? He hid his face in his hands. Then a soft little hand stole over his head and a warm arm about his neck, while in low accents she said :

"Tell me Ben, am I right?"

There was good stuff in those hard-headed and stubborn-minded people who first set Christian foot upon Plymouth Rock. There was good stuff in this their descendant.

He raised his head and taking both of her hands in his, said slowly — even solemnly :

" Yes, darling, you are right! But, oh, you do not know how hard it is to give you up for I love you *so* much! But you are right, God bless you, you are right! The service I rendered was one my manhood owed to humanity — no more. It would ill become that manhood that it claim as a reward that you desert the paths of duty to those loved ones. Kiss me, Bertha; you may do *that*. There now, *sister*, lie down and sleep, for I know you need rest," and he covered her with his coat and piled the leaves and brush about her form.

Then hour after hour Ben sat and held bitter communion with himself.

CHAPTER XXVIII.

DEATH SHAKES HANDS WITH THE CASTAWAYS.

THE castaways arose on the following morning weaker, but refreshed. Their hunger was not so pressing as upon the previous day, but their steps were slower, and their vitality had decreased. No reference was made by either to the conversation of the previous evening. Ben's face wore a look of great sorrow he could not conceal, and Bertha by numerous little attentions and pretty little ways, that are the sole property of her sex, tried to assuage his woes. Alas, the dear girl did not know that the balm she applied to our friend's wounds made them grow the deeper and break out afresh.

Cleveland exerted himself among the cottonwoods and Bertha carried them to the river. During the morning he told her of his own life, and the nature of the tramp that had led him to his present unfortunate position. It was then for the first time she knew that Ben was the boy's champion in Jersey City, and also the stowaway whose passage her intercessions had secured at Columbus. So little had he occupied her attention on those occasions that had he not informed her she would have remained ignorant of the fact that he was Blackoat's antagonist, or the subject of Mr. Blassfeme's aquatic attentions.

" So then our wreck was not your first acquaintance with the river," she said, laughing.

" No," he replied, " that was my second bath."

Later in the day Ben, after both had been for some time engaged in silence at work on the raft, asked suddenly :

" Bertha, what is your cousin's name ? "

" Arthur Blackoat," she replied.

" Arthur Blackoat ! " exclaimed he in a voice of apprehension. " Why — " and then he stopped.

She waited for him to continue, but he said no more, and both resumed their work in silence.

By tearing up one of the young lady's skirts into strips and twisting these, they made cables with which Ben bound the layers of cottonwood firmly together at the corners, and in the centre. The raft being made in the style of a " mattrass " such as the celebrated jettie cribs rest upon at the mouth of the river, and which are to take Nature by the ears and show the old Dame how she should walk the straight and narrow path. Before the middle of the afternoon it would uphold Ben, and by sundown both could safely float upon it.

" We will not start in the dark," said he, " for we need daylight for the attempt, and a breeze that will give us a chance to reach the point below. Early in the morning we will give up Crusoe life, and surrender our domain back to solitude."

Both retired to the hut in high hopes of the morrow's relief, and ere they slept an earnest prayer of thanks for their safety and supplications for the success of their efforts was sent to Him who holds the whole world in the hollow of his hand.

Then they slept — soundly, if not sweetly — for both were exhausted.

Slept — while the great river went rolling by on its way to the sea.

Slept — while from the north, from the east, from the west, from thousands of meadow brooks and mountain torrents, from hundreds of springs and rills, from woodland and from moor, the dragoons of Death rode out on the flood and bore down upon them!

Ben awoke with a cry of alarm. He was wet through, and the floor of their hut was flooded! With wild thoughts surging through his brain and horrible fears palsying his heart, he sprang to his feet and looked out. And there before his eyes, glistening in the morning sunlight, lay one vast expanse of water! The island was already submerged by the flood, *and the raft gone!*

What words can depict the horrors of that moment! Hope? There was no hope, nothing but *despair!* Great, gigantic, crushing despair! Man was powerless — he could not push back the hand of God!

The fall rains had swollen the northern rivers, and they had discharged their superabundance into the Mississippi, and that stream was now rising at the rate of a foot an hour. Already it was over the island and the cottonwood brake stood in a field of water. Ben would have been aroused sooner were it not that he had located his hut on a little knoll in the sand,

higher by a foot than its surroundings. Bertha, re-
posing upon an elevation of boughs within still slept,
but the hungry river was now licking her garments,
impatient for its prey. For an instant he thought to
plunge into the flood and end his miseries at once and
for ever. Then he looked at the sleeping girl and the
prayer sprang to his lips : " Oh God ! Take me but
spare her ! " and kneeling by her side he gazed so
fondly yet so sorrowfully into her face, and then waked
her with a kiss. She looked up with a smile. But
the smile quickly turned to a look of terror, at the
words quietly but earnestly uttered :

" Bertha, we must die. There is no help for us
now. The river is rising. It has covered the island.
Our raft is gone. Death will be upon us soon."

With a wild cry the girl bounded to her feet and
rushed from the hut. The turbid flood stretched all
around her, and she stood in water over her feet.
She turned and looked at Ben, so pityingly, as if for
relief. Oh, the helpless agony of that look ! He
turned away his head with a groan, and did not dare
to look at her again. So he stood, bowed down by
unutterable woe, for some moments ; the cruel waters
steadily and stealthily — oh, how stealthily *creeping,
creeping, creeping*, with a low *plash, plash, plash*, like
the dull senseless whisper of a devil — rising around
him. Then a little hand was placed in his and an
arm laid upon his neck : " Our Father who art in
Heaven, hallowed be thy name. Thy kingdom come
thy will be done — ." He raised his head and looked
at her beside him. There was no fear there now, no
tremor. The face upturned to heaven was the face

of an angel. " Thy will be done on earth as it is in Heaven." Then in a clear, silvery voice, that neither trembled or quavered, the souls of both were confided to the mercy of Him above, and His protection and care invoked for those who should remain upon earth. There was no supplication for life, for all hope now left was a hope for the life immortal. Long did that lovely being appeal to the Most High, and ere she was through, a strange quiet of mind and peace of heart had come to Ben.

When the prayer was ended they locked their arms about one another and stood — waiting for death.

Slowly, but how awfully sure, the waters rose around them. Already the ripples reached their hands as they stood erect. Soon they would be up to their breasts. A slight current was already agitating the eddy that covered the bar, and it caused the tops of the cottonwoods to nod and bend in the water. A little while longer and the current would become a torrent, irresistible in its might and fury. Once she looked up in his face, and said :

" Is it not hard to die, dear friend ? "

And Ben answered : " No, perhaps it is best," and he thought death was a relief. It had lost its terrors and he did not fear it.

" Bertha," he said, " it cannot matter now, — but — it would be a last earthly happiness to me — tell me, do you love me ? "

" With all my heart," she replied.

" God bless you, my darling," he cried.

" God bless us both," she said. " Good-bye," and they kissed one another a last farewell, forever.

Slowly, slowly, oh how terrible and slow, the waters crept, up, up, up! The current grew in strength. The cottonwoods no longer nodded their heads, but bent down in the flood. The feet of the castaways refused their hold upon the crumbling sand. Ben surged with all his strength against the tide. It was of no avail. Their feet slipped from under them. The river grasped them. One piercing shriek, one loud cry — and they were swept away, linked in one another's arms!

CHAPTER XXIX.

THE CRUISE OF THE "ROARER."

IN Bordeaux a man in cap and blouse rolls great wine pipes from great warehouses down to great vessels that lie at the quay. These vessels take the great pipes on board and bear them to the four corners of the earth.

Away up in the wilds of Arkansas a woodman swings his axe, and the great oak topples and falls, with a roll of thunder, to the ground.

The man in the blouse on the docks of Bordeaux has never seen, nor does he know of the existence of the man who swings his axe in the uninhabited timbers of the White River bottoms. They do not speak the same language; they do not worship from the same religion; they know nothing of one another; care nothing. And yet should the woodman stop swinging his axe the man in the blouse would stop rolling barrels; for the iron bands that girt the great wine pipes bind together a mutual interest of these two humble workmen, so many thousand miles apart. And so the woodman in the forest of Arkansas fells the tall white oak for the man in the blouse, in Bordeaux. Tell him so and he will laugh at you. Explain it to him and he will say the reasoning is brought from a distance. But *stop his axe* — and the man in Bordeaux will stop rolling the pipes of wine! For it is the staves from the mighty oak on the White River bottom lands that hold the wine on the docks of Bordeaux.

The stave timber of America is being rapidly exhausted. It has been, and it is a source of much wealth. But a few years ago, Ohio, Indiana and Michigan produced good staves in large quantities. Now their production is very limited, and they have none for export. Indeed they import from other states. A few years ago Northern Michigan sent staves to Cadiz, Spain ; but her timber is rapidly disappearing. The oak forests of Arkansas and Tennessee are still comparatively fresh, and supply many staves to Europe. The most available timber is that located on some of the waterways traversing the forest, on which they may be rafted to the Mississippi or put in flat boats at their " banking " and sent to New Orleans direct. The forest of Eastern Europe, Russia and Hungary, still furnish some staves ; but their trees have been culled over these centuries past, and the New World must be looked to for a steady supply.

The "Mary Jane, No. 2 " had originally left the Virginia shore, a short distance below Wheeling, freighted with jugs and crocks.

The " Mary Jane, No. 2 " was square in front and square behind, and much resembled an enormous drygoods box loaded with pottery. A stovepipe stuck from her deck, " back aft " when that end was up

stream, and "up for'ard" when she had swapped
ends ; which she frequently did.   An oar with a blade
sixteen feet long and a stem fifty feet, hung over the
end opposite the stovepipe.   This was the "gouger.".
A similar one, but with a much shorter stem, hung at
the stovepipe end, and worked, back and forth, above
that article.   That was the " Steer'n o'r."   Two short
heavy-stemmed sweeps, with long blades, were hung
one on each side.   They were all pivoted on iron pins,
and had planks laid on the rounding roof of the craft
for the crew to walk upon as they worked them with
arms extended above their heads.   The three last
named "oars" were not difficult for a stout man to
handle.   But the " gouger," though a child could lift
the stem and dip the blade, would have felled an ox
with the rebound, unless the ox knew how to catch it
and hold it up.

Such was the "Mary Jane, No. 2 "; looking, on
the river, with her long, leg-like sweeps, not unlike a
pre-historic June bug.   From Wheeling to Memphis
she supplied the inhabitants with brown receptacles
for their corn juice, and at Memphis her trip ended
and she was dismantled.   This last being accomplished
by taking the stove out of her " cabin " and remov-
ing the planks of her decking.   Then the " Mary
Jane, No. 2 " lay peacefully soaking in the waters of
Wolf River for many days, until the acquisitive eyes
of Cap'n Willum Smiff, (pronounced with a clear
nose and a mouth unchoked with tobacco-juice, *William Smith*) fell upon her.   When she engaged the
attention of those orbs a change came over the peaceful life of the " Mary Jane."   The name " Mary

Jane, No. 2 " passed into history, and the more robust
and sounding title of " Roarer " adorned her stern.
With the new nomenclature came a new existence.
With Cap'n Willum Smiff at the " steer'n o'r " and
Lieutenant Jeremiah Jarphly at the "gouger " the
" Roarer " sailed for the St. Francis river and was
cordelled a short distance up that stream.   There she
loaded with pipe and barrel staves for the man in the
blouse on the quay in Bordeaux.   The stovepipe was
transferred to the centre of the craft, where it stuck
up belching smoke and fire like a juvenile Popocata-
petl.   Beneath the stack was now a dirty little cabin,
twelve feet square, with bunks on three sides, the
stove in the centre, and a home-made wooden table
with two similarly constructed stools for furniture.
Both cabin and bunks were formed of tiers of staves.
She carried a crew of six men besides Cap'n Willum
Smiff and Lieutenant Jeremiah Jarphly ; and the
" Roarer " cast off her lines and set sail for New Orleans.

When Cap'n Willum Smiff appeared " on deck "
that morning, after a short nap on a coil of rope, he
said " How'dy " to Lieutenant Jarphly and gracefully
tilted a jug to his lips ; the body of the vessel repos-
ing on his elbow — a feat that Cap'n Smiff was quite
proud of.   Then Lieutenant Jarphly tilted it likewise, and as he rubbed his mouth on his shirt sleeve,
said :

" River's risin', Cap'n."

" Yas, by ginger ! " replied Cap'n Smiff.   " Risin'
a boomin', by ginger !   Driftwood comin' down a skal-
lehutin', by ginger !   Whar air we, Jerry ? "

"Wuthin a few miles uv Frenchman's pint," replied his Lieutenant.

"Sho as yoh live, by ginger!" said Cap'n Smiff, and then he and Lieutenant Jarphly took a long and meditative look at the river and their surroundings.

"Jerry, how much's she riz?" presently asked the commander.

"'Bout five fut, I reckon."

"By ginger!"

Then followed another meditation and contemplation.

"Jerry doh yoh know wot I've a mind toh doh?" asked the Cap'n, and Mr. Jarphly confessing an ignorance of his intentions Cap'n Smiff continued:

"I've a right smart notion of tryin' Nigger Head chute!"

"No! Go way!" said Jerry.

"Sho as yoh live, I'll be ginger-gingered to ginger ef I aint! See here, by ginger. Las' time I wus down I noticed a powerful strong kerrent settin' in 'round Frenchman's pint, inter the old channel. 'Taint morn ten yars ago sense we yosed toh go that channel, Jerry. Hit wus right arter the spring flood of sixty-six, when the river cut thro' up at Bordens, thet the kerrent shot off the pint instead of a goin' around hit, an' left thet great, big san' flat thar, five miles wide. Now thet she's bruk thro' onto Hempen's Landin' the kerrent's changin' agin, an' when I kem up on the Bismark frum thet las' trip I was down, I wus up in the pilot house 'long with Jeff Neff, an' I pinted it out to Jeff, an' Jeff sed as how he 'lowed thar'd be the channel agin afore nex' spring! I've a heap mind toh try it; — by ginger!"

But Lieutenant Jarphly was averse to the experiment. For the reason, perhaps, that with nautical prescience, he knew that it involved some extra exertions upon the gouger. The more he objected, however, the more Cap'n Smiff was determined upon the undertaking.

"By ginger! I'll doh it, I swar I will! See here, Jerry, less see wot luck's in hit," and he picked up a broad stave, and expectorating a puddle of tobacco-juice on one side of it, remarked :

"No fur hit, Jerry; chute or no chute — wet or dry? Sing out!" and he whirled the stave in the air.

"Dry!" cried Jerry.

"Wet she is, by ginger!" said Cap'n Smiff, contemplating his sign manual, and little dreaming that the lives of two human beings had hung upon the result.

"*Wet* she is; and the chute we take. *Oars!*"

This last brought the crew from their slumbers to the sweeps, and with steady strokes they commenced propelling the " Roarer " toward the distant point.

"I want toh hug the pint, near as I kin," explained Cap'n Smiff. "Ef we stan' toh fur out the kerrent will take us over to the bend, an' we'll never make the chute."

But the " oars " were well manned and whatever else his ignorance, Captain Smith was a thorough flat boat's man, and understood the river. He certainly ought to have been for from boy to man he had devoted forty years of his life to the study of the science, and all in the world he had to show for it was the greasy clothes on his back. The "Roarer" and cargo belonged to a Memphis firm that employed Cap'n Smiff when he was sober. Still Cap'n Smiff was a happier man, in his way, than many whose possessions are much more extensive. His wants were small, and his vices cheap.

As they hugged the point, he called out to Jarphly:

"Give her the gouger, Jerry!" and two of the crew leaving the sweeps, went to Jerry's assistance, for the gouger was too much for one man.

"Ram hit toh her! Cram hit toh her! Slam hit toh her! Jam hit toh her!" yelled Cap'n Smiff, who was executing a nervous hornpipe with the "steer'n o'r" between his legs.

"She takes hit! Now she takes hit! Thar! That'll do," and the great box swung around the point, and headed for the chute — the first vessel to cruise the old roadway for ten years! *That* was the feather Cap'n Willum Smiff wanted to stick in his nautical cap.

And now that the "Roarer" was headed right, the men bridled their oars and lounged lazily on the staves.

Suddenly one arose with a shout and cried to his companions:

"What's that? Look there! For God's sake, look! Look!"

"Whar?" asked Cap'n Smiff.

"There! There!" and the man's eyes started as he pointed down the chute.

"Great Jehovah!" cried the captain, "Git in the skiff an' go after them, quick, quick!" and before his commands could be executed he himself was seated in the skiff that was being towed along side of the flat boat, and in another moment was shooting down the stream, the boat springing like a race horse under the powerful strokes of his oars. And he was none too quick — none too soon. For as he reached the man and woman clinging together in the center of a sea of waters, their feet went from under them, and the next instant, torn asunder, they would have been beyond the reach of Cap'n Smith's powerful arm. He seized the woman by the hair and dragged her into the skiff, the man clinging to the gunwale until she was safely on board, and then crawling over himself. Both lay in a dead faint on the bottom of the boat, while Cap'n Smiff, with great beads of cold sweat starting from his forehead and rolling down over his furrowed countenance, sat with his arms hanging limp and lifeless by his side, and with eyes blankly staring at the two forms before him, muttered over and over:

"Great Jehovah! Great Jehovah!"

And let you and I, gentle reader, echo the words, though in a different humor:

"Great JEHOVAH!"

CHAPTER XXX.

BEN LOSES HOPE AND TURNS NAVIGATOR.

WHEN the captain regained the "Roarer" and Bertha and Ben were safely stowed in the little stave-cabin, with kind faces bending over and kind hands ministering to them, Cap'n Willum Smiff walked slowly toward Lieutenant Jeremiah Jarphly, and said :

" Jerry, yoh recommember this morn' when we tossed thet thar stave fur the chute or agin hit? "

" Yes."

" Well, Jerry, thet wus a *bowed stave*, an' I spit on the *bowed side* of hit, an' by rights the bowed side oughter hev cum down — but hit did't, Jerry."

" No."

. Then Cap'n Smiff looked hard at his Lieutenant, as though he was trying to shape some unfamiliar thoughts into words.

" No, hit didn't, Jerry. The bent side didn't come down — *it come up*. An' it war agin science, Jerry ; but hit come up an' we tuk toh the chute, an' — an' mought hev sumthin' — thar mought somebody — I dunno — I *swar* I dunno ! " and, as though the unfamiliar thoughts were muddling his brain, Cap'n Willum Smiff walked back to the stem of the "steer'n o'r," and slowly straddling it, deluged his surroundings in tobacco juice, while he lost himself in profound meditation.

There are others than unsophisticated Captain William Smith who have pondered deeply on the same subject, and been lost at sea far from the lighthouse of FAITH.

That evening found the "Roarer" with a line out to a check post on the levee below the city of Vicksburg. On parting from the crew of the flatboat Bertha had distributed all she had of value about her person among them, and bestowed upon Cap'n Smith a glittering diamond cluster ring from off her hand. Cap'n Willum Smiff at first refused to take it, but comprehending that he would hurt the young lady's feelings by refusing longer, he suspended the jewel with a piece of tow about his neck, and vowed that there it should stay 'till death did them part. Alas, for the fragile nature of human vows! In less than a week the diamonds glistened on the person of a New Orleans bar-tender; hypothecated for drinks; while Cap'n Willum Smiff and Lieutenant Jarphly were on one of their "Reg'lar Pelican Sprees! A howlin' Wilderness! You bet!"

After Bertha had been comfortably cared for in bed at the hotel, where she immediately retired under the direction of a physician, Ben, first refreshing himself with a good meal, which she insisted upon his eating, went to the telegraph office and sent the following message to Mr. Charles Braster of the firm of

Braster & Chetwick, Poydras Street, New Orleans:
" Your niece is here safe. Is Mr. Braster in the
city ? " And then with a beating heart he awaited a
reply. For Ben had formed new hopes, and thought
that perhaps the disaster on the Argenta might after
all have been a stroke of good fortune in his favor.
In the course of half an hour an answer was returned,
and as the boy delivered it to him, he had not the
courage to look at it. He unfolded the dispatch,
trembled, then folding it up again without reading,
placed it in his pocket and hastened toward the hotel.
Having walked a block he gained heart, and slowly
taking the dispatch from his pocket, unfolded it and
read :

" Thank God. Arthur and myself are both here
safe. Come down on the Natchez to-night."
(signed)   " CHARLES BRASTER."

That was all. But it was quite enough. His last
hope lay in the dust. " Arthur and myself are here
safe." He read it again as if hoping against hope.
Blackoat was saved ! Blackoat was safe and the idol
of his life had passed from his grasp.

He could not meet her again ; he dared not. Seating himself in the office of the hotel he wrote the following note :

DEAR MISS BERTHA : — I wish you joy. *Both* of
your relatives are safe. Oh, Bertha, I dare not see
you again, my darling, my darling. Pardon my weakness, but if you only knew how sore my heart is you
would pity me. We will probably never meet again.
May your life be one of joy and happiness. You will
do *your* duty nobly — I will, please God, try to do

mine. God bless you, my darling, God bless you. May your future be as full of sunlight as the labor of my life would have made it. Again farewell — Heaven bless you.   BEN."

Having dispatched this to Bertha with the telegram he walked out into the street — again a *tramp*. And a tramp with a sad, sad heart.

It was the last day of September. He was two hundred miles by land and twice as many by river from New Orleans, and had but a day more and a portion of October the 2d to win his wager in. His chances looked desperate. But he was indifferent whether he won or lost. A dull, dead apathy to everything had taken possession of him. He felt that it was a luxury to be a vagabond, an outcast, a tramp, and half inclined not to go to New Orleans at all, but to start off on a roving career, and ramble, ramble, ramble, trying to get away from himself.

" Ye're a stout looking lad; can ye handle a barry ? If ye can I'm taking down a gang of fifty min the night to Burk's work on the levee fifteen mile this side of Baton Rouge, and if yez wants to come along, a dollar a day and four jiggers is the pay," and the stout florid man who addressed him asked:

" Will yez go or not ? Make yer answer quick, for I'm in a hurry."

" Yes, I'm in for a job, and ready," replied Ben, seizing the opportunity to lave Vicksburg.

" Very well," said the man. " Go down and get aboord the Roddy for she'll be laving in an hour. I will see ye on boord and pass yez down."

So on board the Roddy went Ben, and before she

started forty more men engaged for the levee squad
had joined him. In ten minutes' conversation with
these he discovered that not one half of them had any
intention of working on the levee. They were simply
travelling. Some were, like himself, on their way to
New Orleans. Others were off of the great Harvest
Range, and had already stole their way thus far and
were simply " putting in the winter." That is, drifting from place to place as sweet fancy directed them.
They would stop at the levee camp and live off of its
rations until hunted out, after which they would take
up their line of tramping without an object in view
or an ambition to prompt them. As they went down
stream now, so the spring would see them going up,
and the summer months find them scattered through
the northern states. Had one of them been termed
a professional tramp or " dead beat" he would have
repelled the insinuation with indignation. They were
after work but never caught up with it. There were
some Americans in the crowd on the boat but the majority were foreigners.

" Why don't you stay and work at the levee ? "
Ben asked one of them ; " you can earn a dollar a
day at it."

" I'm a brick mason," he replied. " I can not do
levee work. Neither can you, as you'll find out if
you stop and try it."

" But is there no other work save leveeing in the
country ? " asked Ben.

" Oh, yes ; there's cotton picking. Lots of the
bums work all winter at it. They get from seventy-
five cents to a dollar and a quarter a hundred, and can

earn from one to two dollars a day. But the living is beastly! The southern people *mean* well enough, but they have no idea how a laboring man is treated up north, and they use you just the same as they do the niggers; give you rations — a peck of corn meal, five pounds of salt pork and a pound of salt a week. You take this and cook it the best way you can, and sleep in the cotton pen, or any where you please — that's *your* lookout. Working for the niggers, a man gets treated a great deal better than he does working for the white people. The niggers feed you better and they are surer pay."

"What!" cried Ben; "Do the colored people employ white men?"

"*Do* they? Well I should say. Thousands of 'em every winter. A good many of the blacks own land and are well fixed, while nearly all of them that don't own no land of their own, work land on shares."

Ben shortly found a clean spot on the deck and lying down took a much needed sleep.

It was early morning, and still dark, when they disembarked at the camp. The men were all up, however, and as he passed through one of the sheds he had an opportunity for investigating the mysteries of a levee camp. There was not much to see. A long line of rough board bunks, two tier high, were ranged on both sides of the shanty, that was supposed to accommodate four hundred men. That was all. No other furniture, no other necessaries or comfort. Ben thought it a close approach to a stable. Which indeed it was, only the animals cared for were human. While looking about him a bell rang, at sound of

which there was a general cry of "Jiggers! Jiggers!"
and a rush by the four hundred for the outside, where
they surged in impatience about a man mounted on a
barrel, who was dealing out whiskey to them in a small
tin cup. This was the "Jigger boss," and four of
these cupfuls of the liquor were a man's daily rations.

After all had received their jiggers, the cry of
"grub pile! grub pile!" was taken up by the crowd,
and a rush made for a long line of tables standing under another shed. These were loaded with tin plates
and pannikins, iron forks and knives, stacks of snowy
wheat bread, (for the levees have as fine bread as
there is in the country) juvenile mountains of smok-
ing "salt-horse," and immense platters of the fruit
known as the "spud laurel," while great pots of a
dirty brown liquid, facetiously termed "coffee" were
liberally scattered about. This constituted breakfast.
Our hero ate heartily, aided in his gastronomic efforts
by a number of tallow dips stuck in their own grease
along the tables at intervals, and which were continually being knocked over by the banqueters as they
passed along the food. The repast finished Ben went
with the crowd to the levee, just as it became light
enough to see to work. There he became proprietor
of a shovel and wheelbarrow, and was stationed in a
line with twelve others ; similar squads occupying the
levee-line for a distance of half a mile. Scarce had
he thrown three shovels full of dirt into his vehicle,
when a shrill little voice piped out, "up all!" and
the line began to wheel their barrows up a steep incline of planks, on to the broad "dump" that constituted the levee they were building.

"Oye, ye little dyvil, yez is at it airly!" shouted one.

"He haven't a spoonful of dirt in his barry!" said another.

"Be jazez, we'll chuck him into the drink!" said a third.

"And the dyvil fly away wid the bones of the little ferrit!" cried a fourth.

These remarks were directed at a little withered-up old man who was "fore-barrow man," or leader of the gang.

"If McCarty don't take that lad and put him to sturring pots in the soup house, we'll murther him!" exclaimed an exasperated levee builder in the line.

"Can't he purt a dacent man that'll do a dacent day's wurruk in the lade, and not be havin' that canary there killin' of the min wid his 'up alls' an' his own barry without the bottom of it covered?"

"Dyvil blow McCarty and dyvil blow little Dinny, but I'll crish the skull av him in wid a blow of me shovel if he don't be loadin his barry, and not running the feet off av us!"

The little man treated the remarks with dignified indifference, and his "up alls" continued to be a theme of hot maledictions. He was a little used up old levee builder, whose only usefulness now consisted in his being able to hurry the rest of the gang, as a "fore-barrow"; a position that no good laborer would have cared to have filled with the intention of imposing on his co-laborers.

The third time Ben wheeled his "buggy" up the steep incline of planks, he wheeled it off, and both he and the barrow had a fall of six feet much to the hilarity of the gang. This happened to him twice in succession, and as he was ascending the third time off he went, and toppled the plank over with him, bringing three other barrows and their navigators to the ground. A loud howl of execrations greeted this catastrophe. Our hero was called a "watchmaker!" "a flute-player!" "a dancing-master!" "a mud-clark!" "a 'sodden'!" "To go tip the plank over on the min!" "Waz it their loif he waz afther!" "Sure it's graves he should be using his shovel at, and not livyin'!"

The howlings attracted the walking-boss to the spot. "What the dyvil did yez go for to tip the plank over on the min for?" he asked.

Ben replied that it was an accident.

"An occident! Howly Mother! An wazn't the plank afoor yer nose? Would yez want a barn flure to roll the barry on?"

Ben mollified the boss's wrath by telling him of his late shipwreck and the weakness caused thereby.

"Well, ye poor dyvil, yez doan't want to be stoppin' on the livy. Every year there do be rigimints of min that's not fit to shovel sawdust, come tramping along, and aten' the camps up. But you've been missfourtinate. The best yez'll do for yersel will be to get to New Orleans and pick up a job yez 'ud be more used to. Go yez now to the cook's shanty and tell thim to give yez bread and mate; that'll stay by yez till ye make Baton Rouge, and then yez can get on a boat the night and be in New Orleans in the mornin'."

Ben thanked the kind hearted boss, and started down the levee with a big package of bread and " salt-horse " under his arm. He arrived at Baton Rouge, the former capital of the State of Louisiana, after dusk, and during the evening, crawled in among the cotton bales of a Yazoo River stern-wheel freight-boat. No one was on the lookout for passengers, as the boat carried none, so he was left undisturbed, and soon fell into a sound sleep.

Daylight was beaming upon him when he was awakened by a rough shake.

" Git up boss, git up.   We muss have dis yere bale ob cotton ! "

He awoke to find the boat stopped, and a gang of black long-shore men unloading her.

" Where am I ? " he asked.

" Whare are yere ?   Why yere at New Orl'ns, ob course ! "

New Orleans !

The tramp was done !

The wager won !

New Orleans !

CHAPTER XXXI.

NEW ORLEANS, 10 A. M., OCT. 2D.

OUR hero could scarcely realize that he was at last in New Orleans. That New Orleans, so pregnant with his hopes and attainings. New Orleans, his thought by day and dream by night. New Orleans, the first accomplishment of his life!

Yet so it was. He was safely landed in New Orleans, and it was the morning of the second of October!

"What time is it?" he asked, as he sprang on shore.

"Nine o'clock," replied a gentleman looking at his watch.

Nine o'clock! And at *ten* o'clock Smythe would be awaiting his telegram in New York City!

Twenty thousand dollars, fairly won! And then came a dull, dead pain that nipped his exultations. What if it were twenty times twenty thousand dollars? The money could not give him happiness. He had lost what money could not recover. What was the vile stuff but a tantalization? An allurement that promised everything and was empty of fulfillments?

Hold on, friend Ben, don't speak disrespectfully of money. Money is the lever that moves the world, and love the fulcrum it rests upon. Had you a fortune would not the lady of your affections be within your reach? Is she not *selling* herself to Arthur Blackoat, and would she not much rather effect the sale with you? The sale is to be a sacrifice, Ben, a sacrifice — the highest bidder takes her.

Then a great flash of hope illuminated his countenance. She had confessed she loved him. Aye, had given herself to him, and he had sacrificed her himself on the altar of Mammon for the good of her mother and that little bed-ridden sister. But circumstances were altered. He was now possessed of a small fortune. Twenty thousand dollars awaited his call in New York City, while four hundred, had, per agreement, been sent to a correspondent at New Orleans and was now subject to his order. Twenty thousand four hundred dollars! It was quite a sum of money. Twenty thousand dollars, judiciously invested, would afford an income of twelve or fifteen hundred dollars per annum. Enough for two persons to live quite comfortably on. He would give the whole of it to Bertha's mother and sister. He would present them with the twenty thousand dollars, and keeping the four hundred for a start in life, marry the girl he loved and be happy.

Remember, gentle reader, Ben was young and sanguine, and *unmarried*. His mother-in-law, at the time, was in embryo. We older heads look at these things differently.

What a wonderful change the face of nature wore

after these bright hopes and satisfactory intentions had possession of him. Everything was light, airy, joyous, happy. He could fairly have shouted aloud in the fullness of his heart, and offered up many a mental thanksgiving as he hurried up Canal Street. Had his feelings not been so surcharged with resurrected hopes he might have noticed that he was on the handsomest thoroughfare in the world. A street that has not its equal in any city on the globe. The beauties of architecture that line it are not prominent (with the exception of one of the most ornate pieces of iron architecture in America, that stood at the foot of it and in the very centre of the street. It is now demolished, but a few years ago was one of the curiosities of the city.) It is not the buildings that make Canal Street the thing of beauty it is, but it is the great, wide picturesque street itself, with its tramways and grass-plots and trees and *banquettes* in the very centre of it, and its broad roadways on each side. A noble artery for the great city.

But Ben cared little about streets or cities just then. His mind and body were alive with new projects for a gladsome future. He passed a jeweller's and learned the time. It was exactly twenty-five minutes past nine. The time was exact. Regulated to a second from the observatory at Washington daily. In five minutes more he had turned down St. Charles Street and entered the rotunda of the St. Charles hotel. He quivered with suppressed excitement as he wrote :

" New Orleans, Oct. 2d, 9.30 A. M., St. Charles Hotel.

"*I am here. Answer immediately.*
"Benjamin Cleveland.
"To Algernon Smythe, Esq., Park Row, New York City."

When he had handed this to the operator, and seen him tick it off upon his wonderful little instrument, he felt quieter, and sat down to await the reply.

We will not attempt to depict Ben's thoughts as he sat there. Suffice it for us to know that they were one great swell of triumph, and the pictures of future happiness that floated before his fancy were gorgeous with crimson and gold. Just as the hands of the clock announced ten o'clock, the operator called to him, and with the remark that the matter had been expeditiously attended to, handed him the following dispatch:

"Park Row, New York City, }
         October 2d, 10.45 A. M. }
"Dear boy, we all sympathize with you. Your dispatch came to hand fifteen minutes ago. You have lost by thirty minutes. Money has been paid to Smythe.
"John Hough, stake-holder.
"Augustus Wasson, referee."

Ben read it, and reread it, and read it over and over again. The date caught his eye, "10.45 A. M." He looked at the clock in the rotunda; it was but ten o'clock and five minutes then. He called the operator's attention to it.

"Oh, yes; you see the difference between New York and New Orleans time is sixty-two minutes. When it is nine-thirty *here*, it is a little past *ten-thirty there.* A great many people who don't think of this, are surprised to receive dispatches ahead of time, as they think. And it's laughable to see their astonishment sometimes." And the clerk laughed in verification of it.

But Ben heard him not. His mind was in a whirl. His body trembled. His legs refused their support and he would have fallen to the floor had not an attendant caught him.

" You 'pears to be sick, sah. Bettah take some fresh air, sah."

" Lost! Lost! Lost!" he cried. "Everything LOST!"

CHAPTER XXXII.

THE LITTLE PARTNER.

IT was a lovely sunny afternoon, two days after the occurrence narrated in the preceding chapter. Canal Street was crowded with the wealth and beauty and fashion of the Crescent City. Fair-haired daughters of the North swept by in pleasing contrast to the black-eyed beauties of the far South. Men lounged through the crowd who looked like pictures from some old canvas ; with dark, swarthy, oval faces, and eyes of midnight darkness. The delicate physique of the octoroon, the creamy tint of a still lighter-tainted blood, the voluptuous forms of the griff, the olive-hued creole, and the clear pink and white of the Anglo-Saxon southron, blended in an ever-moving, ever-shifting panorama of life that entranced the eye and bewildered the sense of the stranger within the city's gates.

A tall, square-shouldered, handsome young man floated along in the living stream. He was dressed in the height of fashion, yet with the pleasing restrictions of good taste and good sense. He strolled along with the easy careless step of one accustomed to seeing and being seen. Many were the admiring flashes dark voluptuous eyes cast upon him, many the smiles he received. But he paid but little heed to the homage. His face, though bronzed, was pale, and there was a weary, restless, unsatisfied look in his eye that illy comported with his bearing.

It was our friend, Benjamin Cleveland, rehabilitated, revamped, repolished, reset, rehumanized, and restored to society. So much for good clothes. Clothes do not make the man, but a man is unmade without them. They introduce him to society and keep him in it afterward. We like to rebel against their tyranny, and say contemptuous things about them, but we fear, honor, and obey them all the same. It is a pity he could not have clothed that restless, unsatisfied eye. For it but too plainly indicated that our hero's thoughts were not pleasant or satisfactory ones. Which indeed they were not, for at that identical moment Ben was wishing himself at the Hotel de Log, in the old livery of poverty and trampdom, and the old liberty of vagabondage. He sighed for the "footpath." He longed to be a *tramp* again. His good clothes felt queer and uncomfortable. They were shackles upon his actions. He did not possess them, but they possessed him. In his rags he could have sat on the curbstone and taken a rest, with no one to give him particular notice. He dared not do it now. As a tatterdemalion he could have stuck his hands in his pockets, leaned against a lamppost with crossed legs and enjoyed the scene. Now — he was on exhibition himself. The first night he attempted to sleep in a bed he laid awake a long time, and ultimately had to get up and roll himself in a blanket on the floor, with the washbasin for a pillow, before sleep would come to him. He had no hopes, no aspirations, no promptings to be or to do. He seriously thought of resuming tramping as a profession. A panacea for a mind diseased. A balm for the wounds of his disappointments. A trunk full of his clothing had been forwarded to New Orleans, and his wardrobe was satisfactory. He had four hundred dollars in his pocket. All the money he had in the world. What was he to do? He did not know, and did not care. He had lost the woman he loved — for whom had he to labor? Himself? Bah! The "foot-path" was a luxury and a release. He was half inclined to lock his trunk and send it to some charitable institution for the benefit of the inmates, go on one tremendous spree with his four hundred dollars, and when the last cent was used up start out on the tramp.

While these thoughts were looking out of his eyes he nearly ran against a ragged boy, who was lounging on the sidewalk.

"Why, Tommy!" he cried in surprise. "You here in New Orleans!"

But Tommy drew back and looked at him distrustfully.

"Why Tom, don't you know me? Are you going back on an old friend? I am Ben, your old friend Ben."

"I'll — be — blowed!" and Tommy said no more, but gazed upon him in astonishment.

"Come Tommy, shake hands, little partner."

"Great guns! The prodigal's got home, the calf's

been slaughtered, he's got his ring on, and — Ben *is* it you ?"

" Me for a fact, Tommy. Do I look so much altered ? "

" *Altered!* Why you are a regular *swell.* Who'd ever think you'd been a tramp !" and Tommy was again lost in astonishment. Then in the old familiar tone, he said, seizing Ben's hand and caressing it in his own peculiar way, " but I'm so glad Bennie, *so* glad you are in luck. Do you live here ? Do your folks live here ? "

" No, Tommy dear, I do not live here nor have I any relatives here — nor am I in luck. But never mind that, I want you to come with me and get a new suit of clothes."

" Oh, never mind my togs, Ben, these will do very well," and Tommy blushed, and laughed a little. "This suit I'm used to and it *suits* me. I want you to walk over there to a bench in the park, and we will sit down and have a long chat."

After they had seated themselves the boy said:

" I never expected to see you again, Ben, and I've cried night after night thinking about you. I thought you were drowned. When we were thrown into the water I caught hold of a spar, but a piece of timber struck against it and knocked me off. I got hold of the timber, however, and was picked up by another boat, an Arkansas River packet, and brought clear down here. Now tell me how it all happened with you."

Ben related the adventures already known to the reader and moreover told Tommy of the object of his tramp to New Orleans, and how he had lost his wager.

"It's all up with me now, Tom," said he sorrow-fully. "I have a great mind to put on the old clothes, and you and I will go tramping again."

"No, no, Bennie, *don't* do that. Do something no-ble and worthy of yourself. You are young, the world is before you; it has honors and happiness for those who earn them; be true to yourself, Ben, dear. *Don't* sink to the horrid level of an outcast, a tramp, when you may live to honor yourself and do good to your fellowmen."

Ben gazed at him in blank amazement. He could not believe his ears.

"Tommy, what — what in the world's come over you? You speak like — like the top line of a copy book!"

"Ben," and he gently laid a hand on Ben's arm; "Ben, I speak what I feel. I like you, Ben — more than you know or understand. I want to see you worthy of yourself, so that I may be proud of you. And then, sometime, maybe, when the little tramp comes to you and says: 'Hi, Bennie, old boy; re-member old times?' you'll think kindly of your little partner — that once was — perhaps, maybe, you'll love him, just a little bit, for the sake of old times, and — and — "

"Why Tommy, what are you crying about? My dear boy, there's something wrong with you. Tell me what it is. If money can be of any assistance, Tom, I've four hundred dollars and you're welcome to the whole of it."

"No, no, Ben," said Tommy, checking his tears,

"I do not want money. I — I want you to like me Ben — to — to — Ben, I haven't any one to *love* me!" and the tears came again.

"There, there, my dear boy, don't give way that way. I love you, Tommy, and I always will. Why little one, I have nobody to love me. I'm alone in the world myself. And — and — "

"'And' what, Ben?"

"And I always expect to be," he concluded bitterly.

"Oh, you will find some one to love, Benjamin," said the lad more cheerfully. "Where there's a Jack there's a Jill, you know. And didn't you improve the chances of your wreck on the sandbar? I thought you were smitten, Ben?"

"Hold on, Tommy. Don't speak that way. I love that dear girl more than words can express. She is an angel, Tom, and — "

"Oh, bah! Angel nothing. She's just a pretty, simpering, bread-and-butter do-nothing — "

"Tommy, stop! I won't have it. I will not allow you to speak so of that young lady."

"But I say she is. She's a flirt! She just is and nothing more!"

"Why Thomas, what in the name of Heaven has come over you? You look and speak so strange. You vilify this young lady whom you do not know, and whom I so love. You — "

"She ain't worthy of you, Ben, indeed and 'deed she aint," and Tommy's voice softened and the tears commenced to flow again.

Ben looked at him anxiously. He is sick, he

thought. Troubles and privations and the terrors of the wreck on the river have exhausted and worried him into illness.

" Poor, little fellow," said he, putting his arm about the boy's body and drawing him close to him. " You aint well, Tommy, and I know it. There, there — never mind what you said. I know you meant nothing rude. You are only mistaken, Tommy. Bertha is one of the noblest girls that lives. Why do you know she is about to marry a man, whom I know she despises, so that she can give her widowed mother and poor bed-ridden little sister a home?"

"No! Is that so?" and Tommy stared incredulously at Ben.

"It is Tommy. She is to marry her cousin to secure a home for her mother and sister," and Ben related to the boy what Bertha Ford had told him relative to her uncle's will.

"And *he*, does *he* love her?"

"From the conversation we both overheard in Pittsburg I should say not. I think he only marries her to secure the money."

" Her fate will be *terrible*," and the boy shuddered.

" Terrible indeed, Tommy. We speak about women *selling* themselves, who of us knows the fearful yet noble sacrifices they may be making in their sale?"

" Good, Ben, good! That shows your heart in the right place, my boy, and please God it stay there," said Tommy, very earnestly. " But she little knows the man she is about to marry."

" Do *you* know him, Tom?"

" Ben," said the boy speaking sharp and quick,

"Listen to me before I change my mind. What you have told me has — has altered some intentions of my own. You love this girl ; does she love you? "

" I *know* she does."

" Very well. Now don't ask me a question ; don't say a word to me. There is to be a wedding to-morrow at St. Martin's Church, Georges Street. *Her* wedding. You attend it. *Don't fail.* You shall have her. *I, Tommy, your little tramp friend, will make her your wife;* but — oh, Bennie, Bennie — " and frantically throwing his arm's around Ben's neck, he kissed our hero's lips, and breaking from him, rushed away.

Long, Ben sat, lost in astonishment. Stupefied. Then he slowly made his way back to his hotel.

CHAPTER XXXIII.

IN AT THE DEATH.

S T. Martin's Church did not wear a very festival
appearance. It looks more like a funeral than
a marriage, that is about to take place, said Ben to
himself, as he quietly entered that edifice on the following morning and seated himself in the dark corner
of a dark pew, where he could observe what transpired without being himself noticed.

A few idlers, evidently people who seeing a church
door open thought it as good a place to sit down and
rest as any that would offer, dropped in and sat in the
rear seats. One had several bundles, evidently a
clerk taking a purchase to the home of a customer
who sought the opportunity to rest his arms and legs
among the cushions of St. Martin's. Some well
dressed people, probably strangers in the city, sat in
respectful silence while they examined the edifice with
their eyes. A country couple chatted pleasantly together, and now and then indulged in a little laugh,
followed by a great deal of whispering. Near them a
man sat down with a large paper of peanuts, which he
was contentedly devouring when the sexton politely

suggested that he either put them up or swallow the shells.

It was evidently to be a private affair. The church was dark and gloomy, and only the shutters of the chancel windows were opened, throwing a faint, mysterious light upon the long queer-looking line of empty pews.

Presently the officiating minister entered the chancel from a door in the rear, clothed in his long white surplice, and sat down while his eyes investigated the inside of a prayer-book, and kept glancing over the top of it and down the main aisle as though impatient for their coming. Then the sound of wheels were heard without, the organ startled those within by breaking out in a peal of sacred melody, and through the open doors came the bridal party. Bertha leaned on the arm of her uncle. She was dressed richly, but quietly, in a travelling suit, as though the intention was to commence the wedding tour at the chancel railing. She was very, very pale, and the great, glorious, grey eyes seemed to cover her whole face, and looked *black* in their intensity. But her head was erect and her step firm. She knew what she was doing, she had counted the cost. She was accepting a lifetime of misery that she might give a home to those she loved. Ben's breath came short and thick, and his hands worked nervously as his eyes were fastened upon her. An elderly lady, the aunt of Miss Ford, was brought in on the arm of Arthur Blackcoat. Blackcoat looked triumphant. He was a trifle pale, and his swarthy countenance in the dim light looked sallow. But his dark eye flashed out the " success " that was crowning his desires, and he looked impatient for the ceremony to proceed. A dozen ladies and gentlemen, friends of the Brasters, had entered the church with them, and among them Ben was surprised to see none other than Mr. Jonah Nipper, in company with a very well dressed dignified gentleman of middle age. These two sat a little apart from the rest.

Presently Bertha Ford and Arthur Blackcoat stood at the chancel railing alone and the beautiful marriage service of the Episcopal Church was commenced by the officiating clergyman.

Ben could hardly comprehend what was taking place; could hardly realize that the woman he so adored was being every moment separated farther and farther from him by a chasm that could never be bridged over for his hopes to cross on. Then his ears caught the solemn words :

" Into this holy estate these two persons come now to be joined. If any man can show just cause why they may not be lawfully joined together let him now speak or else hereafter forever hold his peace."

Cleveland could hardly restrain himself from shouting out :

" I do ! The woman loves *me !* "

Bah, Ben. Don't make a fool of yourself. *That* is not a "*just cause.*"

There being no interruption the clergyman continued :

" I require and charge you both, as ye will answer at the dreadful day of judgment, when the secrets of all hearts shall be disclosed, that if either of you

know any impediment why ye may not be lawfully
joined together in matrimony ye do now confess it.
(Blackoat was steadying himself with one hand on
the chancel railing.) For be ye well assured that if
any persons are joined together otherwise than as God's
word doth allow their marriage is not lawful."

Blackoat released the railing and stood erect, but
his face was very pale and his eyes rested steadily on
his feet. Turning to him the minister asked :

" Wilt thou have this woman to be thy wedded
wife, to live together after God's ordinance in the
holy state of matrimony? Wilt thou love her, comfort her, honor her and keep her in sickness and in
health, and forsaking all others keep thee only unto
her, so long as ye both shall live ? "

And Blackoat answered :

" I will."

" You lie ! "

The words rang out clear and sharp. They re-
sounded through the edifice. Echoed along the gal-
leries. Rebounded back from the chancel, and filled
the whole interior with a cold, metallic startling ring.
All present sprang to their feet and looked in amazement down the main aisle. Blackoat, of all there,
did not turn his head. Had he been cast of bronze
he could not have been more motionless, more dead.

" Who interrupts the ceremony ? " asked the minister recovering from his surprise.

" *I do !* " and a lithe form in male attire bounded
up the aisle and stood in front of the chancel rail.
"I do ! His Lawful Wife ! "

It was Tommy !

To his dying day Ben will never forget the horror his eyes then saw. The church had the stillness of death. Not a muscle moved of those there gathered. Eyes starting from their sockets reached for the mass at the chancel rail, but motion there was none. All might have been chiselled out of stone. Pale as death the figure clad in male attire stood between the woman and man, a hand extended repelling the one, a hand upraised denouncing the other, two glittering brown eyes fastened on the man's face. And the man — slowly he turned upon his feet, as though some mechanism moved an inanimate object. Slowly came he round and faced the glittering eyes. *The eyes of the dead!* And as he faced them the sallow of his countenance turned to the white of clay, his jaw dropped upon his breast, revealing, in ghastly display, his white teeth. And up, up, up, from the ground came his eyes, until they rested on the white face before him. Then in a yell that called a responsive shriek from all present, *he* shrieked, " GOD AL-MIGHTY ! " and fell back — DEAD.

CHAPTER XXXIV.

CONCLUSION.

READER, we thank you for your kind attention. Our tale is told, and we shall impose upon it but a moment longer. It would not probably interest you to know that the twenty thousand dollars worth of forged notes, forged by the dead man, still remain in the hands of Mr. Jonah Nipper — and are likely so to do for all time to come. During the first three years of their married life, Ben and his beautiful wife received a letter without a signature. It told of a young girl that had been betrayed by a heartless man, and persuaded by him to leave her humble home. Harassed by her importunities in a moment of weakness to his cold, crafty self, he had allowed a marriage ceremony to be performed. Shortly after, the man's uncle died leaving provisions in his will that made the man *hate* the poor helpless being he found himself tied to. Her death was his only release. A dark night on a Hudson River steamer, a blow and a splash in the waters, and he thought himself a free man. But the girl lived. Lived to hunt him down with the fury of a tigress.

In poverty she pursued her revenge. As a tramp, in
male attire, she tracked her would be murderer. At
last revenge seemed to come within her reach. She
would wait until he had violated the law, and then
crush him and his hopes, as a bigamist. But meanwhile the love that had died blossomed anew. She
thought to live and love once more. It was not to be.
The object of her new love had given his heart to another. Still she loved him, and as a last offering of
her love placed within his reach the idol of his heart,
all unsullied.

Both Bertha and Ben strove to discover her where-
abouts. From that day to this, " *Tommy* " has been
neither seen nor heard of by them. They live in all
the luxury wealth can offer. As happy as happy can
be. Smythe, Hough and Wasson were at the wedding, and all claim to have provided Ben with this
terrestrial paradise by sending him on that trip to
New Orleans. The Cleveland's house is known to
the fraternity of the foot-path far and wide. There
is not a vagabond of them but knows that a hearty
meal and substantial help await all who knock at that
door. And their calls are numerous and frequent.

www.ingramcontent.com/pod-product-compliance
Lightning Source LLC
Chambersburg PA
CBHW030343270326
41926CB00009B/944